T0194842

FROM **HELL** TO
REBIRTH

A True Story of Long-Term Suffering with Chronic Illness,
Addiction, and Lyme Transformed by the Will to Live

MICHELLE L. POTTER

BALBOA.PRESS
A DIVISION OF HAY HOUSE

Balboa Press books may be ordered through booksellers or by contacting:

Balboa Press
A Division of Hay House
1663 Liberty Drive
Bloomington, IN 47403
www.balboapress.com
844-682-1282

Because of the dynamic nature of the Internet, any web addresses or links contained in this book may have changed since publication and may no longer be valid. The views expressed in this work are solely those of the author and do not necessarily reflect the views of the publisher, and the publisher hereby disclaims any responsibility for them.

The author of this book does not dispense medical advice or prescribe the use of any technique as a form of treatment for physical, emotional, or medical problems without the advice of a physician, either directly or indirectly. The intent of the author is only to offer information of a general nature to help you in your quest for emotional and spiritual well-being. In the event you use any of the information in this book for yourself, which is your constitutional right, the author and the publisher assume no responsibility for your actions.

Any people depicted in stock imagery provided by Getty Images are models, and such images are being used for illustrative purposes only.
Certain stock imagery © Getty Images.

Print information available on the last page.

ISBN: 978-1-9822-5584-8 (sc)
ISBN: 978-1-9822-5585-5 (hc)
ISBN: 978-1-9822-5610-4 (e)

Library of Congress Control Number: 2020919225

Balboa Press rev. date: 09/29/2020

DISCLAIMER

The information provided in *From Hell to Rebirth* is for informational and educational purposes only. The author, Michelle L. Potter, is not a licensed medical doctor and does not offer medical, psychological, or any other professional advice that prescribes or provides any type of medical diagnosis, treatment, medications, cures for disease, or remedies that can only be given by a licensed medical doctor.

Statements made in this book have not been evaluated by the U.S. Food & Drug Administration (FDA). You should always consult and seek the advice of a qualified health care practitioner with any questions you might have regarding your medical condition or as it specifically relates to any protocols that the author discusses about her own journey with addictions, chronic illness, and Lyme Disease.

Some names and identifying details have been changed to protect the privacy of individuals.

DEDICATION

First, and above all, I would like to thank God. You have given me the power to believe in my passion, pursue my dreams, and open and close doors that only You can open and close. You carried me when I needed carrying, you walked beside me when I needed assistance, and you comforted me even in the darkest hours, in the pits of hell, when I wasn't being obedient. You gave me strength and courage to write this book, to be vulnerable, and to be a voice for others who cannot speak for themselves. I have been redeemed, forgiven, and saved from the enemy's hit on my life. Thank you for keeping me here on Earth longer to fulfill your work of serving and helping others to heal from their life experiences, traumas, and illnesses. I am forever grateful and will glorify and honor You until you bring me home to the heavens.

To my heart and world, Steve, Brynin, and Kylie. I am one blessed wife and momma. Writing this book has been extremely difficult—reliving the past, letting go, and being present in the moment. But it's been necessary for healing and rewarding all at the same time. None of this would have been possible without the support, care, encouragement, laughter, and unconditional love you gave me. You never wavered on believing and loving me—from my brightest days to my darkest hours. Every day is about going on new adventures and making new memories together. For that I am forever grateful! Forever Stars and Moon!

Your life is a sacred journey.
And it is about change, growth, discovery, movement, transformation,
continuously expanding your vision of what is possible, stretching your
soul, learning to see clearly and deeply, listening to your intuition, taking
courageous challenges at every step along the way. You are on the path...
exactly where you are meant to be right now... And from here, you
can only go forward, shaping your life story into a magnificent tale of
triumph, of healing of courage, of beauty, of wisdom, of power, of dignity,
and of love.
~ Caroline Adam

CONTENTS

CHAPTER 1

THE BEGINNING

We must know who we are and where we are.
~ Donna Goddard

I was born and raised in the small town of Gibson, Louisiana, a community in Terrebonne Parish, and our house sat right across the street from a Louisiana bayou called Bayou Black. The bayou led out to the Intracoastal Waterway, which connected to the Atchafalaya River, which eventually poured into the Gulf of Mexico. That's the route my parents would take to go shrimping, and I would sometimes go with them. The swamp was literally in our backyard, and the mosquitoes were so plentiful they could almost carry you away at night. The sound of rain frogs and bullfrogs filled the air at night, too, and alligators swam in the bayou and made their homes in the ditches.

My grandparents on my mom's side lived next door to us—"us" being my mom and dad and my sister, Shanna, and my brother, Jesse— and my other set of grandparents lived about ten minutes away. Since my parents were away from home a lot—they'd be on their boat, shrimping, all through May and August—I'd spend many days over at the house of Maw Maw and Paw Paw, my mom's parents. In fact, any time I didn't want to be at my parents' house—and there were many—I'd head over across the yard to spend time with Maw Maw, mostly. By the time I was four or five, Maw Maw and Paw Paw started taking me camping with them for a weekend or so. That's when I discovered my love of nature.

I never wanted to be inside if I didn't have to be. Being inside felt like a prison to me sometimes; I just loved being outdoors too much. Nature nurtured me and provided me with a sense of calmness. It was just so soothing to my soul. The earthy, grounding sensation I got from the outdoors lifted my spirits and connected me to something bigger than myself. I loved being barefoot, rolling around in some mud so much that I got into a lot of trouble because I refused to keep shoes on my feet. It really was my happy place.

We had lots of animals hanging around with us when I was growing up. You'd find dogs, goats, rabbits, chickens, ducks, owls, and even a pet nutria, which looks a little like a small beaver. On our street, everybody considered our house the animal drop-off place. But both my mom and I loved rescuing animals—it was one of the few things we shared and continue to share to this day. We'd get stray dogs coming by and staying around, and we'd make little sweaters and little hats for them so they'd stay warm. I loved sitting outside with them. They all wanted to sit in my lap and have me hold them.

All of my animals had names; my favorite chicken was named Babe. I took her everywhere with me, carrying her around on my hip like a baby. But my sworn enemies were the roosters. They would chase me around my grandparents' yard, and my Maw Maw would have to come out of the house with her broom to keep them from attacking me.

All the animals felt like a huge cup of love to me. I felt they understood me, and I understood them, too. In a very real way, they were my little family; they were all my babies that I could love unconditionally, and I'd get it all back in return and then some.

Being the firstborn, I grew up very quickly. By the time I was five, I was washing dishes, cleaning, cooking, and helping mom around the house. Jesse and Shanna insisted that I was bossy and mean sometimes as we grew older, but the way I see it, I threw myself into the role of parenting them soon after they arrived on the scene. I had spent four years as an only child by the time my brother was born, so it took me a while to adjust to my new reality. But then a switch went off, and I stepped into something of a parenting role that seemed to resonate for me. My mom tells me I started walking around with the attitude: "He belongs to me now, and I'm going to take care of him."

Call it what you might, I was always making sure that my siblings were in check. After all, I figured, no matter who was actually doing the troublemaking, we would all get in trouble for it. So, I tried to stay one step ahead of what could happen, playing different scenarios in my head, people-pleasing when necessary, trying to prevent any repercussions from something bad that might happen. Unfortunately, it didn't always work out. And then, I'd take it all very seriously, analyze the situation and try to figure out what I did wrong, taking the blame as if it was my fault that things didn't work out better for the three of us. Trying to protect my siblings and myself.

We had a lot of cousins, too. Sometimes they were around so much it felt like they were just another set of siblings—they just happened to live in the city and not the country like we did. Once the cousins arrived at Maw Maw's, they would always gravitate next door to our house to come and play. For that reason, our house was nicknamed the "magnet" house. We'd often play and hang out together on weekends and at the holiday gatherings my Maw Maw loved to put together. She loved to cook and entertain, so she'd create lots of gatherings for us. Whether it was Christmas, Thanksgiving, Fourth of July, Easter, or the Blessing of the Fleet, we'd all be together.

The Blessings of the Fleet, a yearly tradition, would occur one to two weeks before the shrimping season opened. Our priest from church would stand on the dock and bless the decorated boats passing by.

Afterward, there would be a celebration with live music, food, games for the children, and a volleyball tournament. Everyone had a good time. After a few years, it came to an end because so many people attended, and the liability risks were too much to bear.

While there were many good times and lots of memories for most of us, and while cherished traditions were passed down, most of the time, there was a lot of outright conflict. Anger and hatred just seemed to bubble up into some sort of violent exchange. My mom and her siblings did not get along at all. Period. Yet everyone would put on a smile, trying to pretend that they liked each other. I hated every minute of it. I would just sit there, not saying much, trying to make sense of it all in my own little world.

It went on like that for years, and, unfortunately, it still continues to this day.

I spent a lot of time with my dad's side of the family, too. Grandpa called me Mitch, and I loved listening to his war stories. He loved to piddle around with his special treasures around his house, especially if they had to do with tractors and the farm life. He loved to put on old music and dance. Grandma had the most beautiful skin and hair. She taught me about skincare and how to always make sure my face was protected from the sun. "Don't forget to moisturize!" she'd say. She and I would have long, deep conversations about life and its struggles, which I will always treasure.

I loved spending time with my two aunts, Joyce and Julie, too, when they visited. They gave me the rare experience of feeling special, as they curled my hair, put makeup on me, and let me wear their clothes. It made me feel like a model.

Besides these more intimate moments, I witnessed events in the neighborhood that seemed to come close to threatening World War III. People in the neighborhood had their conflicts and couldn't stop themselves from expressing intense anger, jealousy, and even outright hatred towards each other. Many horrible incidents resulted from people lashing out at each other, causing tremendous pain and hurt on both sides.

One time, when my parents were away, two people we knew were over, visiting, and started to scream profanities at each other. It ended in a fistfight in the middle of the yard. Then, one of them turned to me, screaming, "You like what you see? You want some of this, too?" It was one of many explosive episodes witnessed.

Of course, I didn't tell my parents about what happened because I didn't want to be a tattletale. I just bottled it up inside me. I didn't want to get in trouble with anyone else. Besides, my parents weren't getting along very well with the people in question, either. If I had told them what happened every time there was a blow-out around us, it would only have added fuel to the fire. It's not like I had good news when I came in saying, "Hey, guess what happened this weekend!"

Another time, someone else we knew showed up at my parents' house with a baseball bat and threatened to kill my daddy. He stood there and yelled for us to come out, commanding that we watch while he smashed my daddy's head in with his baseball bat. I remember crying and praying that my daddy would not be hurt and that such an evil person and his psychotic episodes would go away and never come back. Unfortunately, he came back many more times.

It wasn't a great environment for a kid to grow up in.

As I continued to be a witness to so much discord and hurt, my own anger, bitterness, resentment, hatred, confusion and fear started to build within me. I started developing my own inner discord. Yet I rarely, if ever, shared all of the trauma I was experiencing with anyone.

On top of all that, my mom was over-protective of me. Maybe it was because I was the firstborn that my mom worried and overreacted at just about everything I did or wanted to do. She wouldn't let me go anywhere, either; I lived a sheltered life. Later, she'd let my younger sister and brother get away with just about everything compared to all the things she didn't let me do. They didn't have all the rules I had to live by. All the way into high school, my mom wouldn't let me do what most of the other high school kids were doing. I had a 10 o'clock curfew—even on special occasions, like prom and homecoming that went until midnight—and lived 30 minutes away from the nearest town. I'd be lucky just to be allowed to go to the movie theatre and a dinner.

It wasn't until much later, when I wanted to move to Alabama to transfer between colleges, that my daddy put his foot down, saying it was time for me to be free. "This child needs to go," he told her. "She is almost 21 years old. She needs to leave, spread her wings, and go do something for herself." I was finally free. But it wasn't easy. While I tried to navigate the real world in a whole new way—without rules and curfews, making my own choices and making new friends—my mother was having a meltdown at the nearby Holiday Inn, worrying about my safety in an unfamiliar place.

Because of our differences and all the rules that she imposed on me when I was growing up, my mom and I had an extremely difficult relationship. We fought a lot. She was raised to believe that if one person was hurting, then they get to make the other person hurt, too—not realizing that life or death is in the power of the tongue. They could say whatever they wanted to the other person's face, no matter how hurtful it might be. Then they'd wait a while for it to blow over and then pretend nothing ever happened. But that never worked for me. The insults were extremely painful and hurtful, which only allowed more anger, bitterness, and resentment to build in my soul. My body was only keeping score. I felt powerless with no voice. When I did have a voice, there were always repercussions that followed. So, the next best thing to do was to stay silent.

I cried a lot. It didn't help that I seemed to have certain facial expressions that got me into deeper trouble. Without saying a word, something about the way that I looked at her made her angry. It would not end well. Many hurtful words were exchanged from both of us.

"The two of us were like oil and water," my mom told me recently, and she was right. I had a free spirit and needed to be outside experiencing life, and she wanted to keep me safe.

My mom has always been very fearful. Just recently she told me that, when she was a little girl, she heard things and saw things that no one else did. She saw ghosts and heard voices coming in through the window of her bedroom, and she'd run into her parent's room at night and tell them that she was seeing scary things. They'd just say, "No, you're not. Now, go back to bed." After a while, her father got so frustrated with her that he got some planks of wood and blocked off her whole window, saying, "See? Now, nobody can come in your room." She seems to have carried that fear all the way into her adult life. And it's probably why she wouldn't accept the fact that I experienced the same kind of thing when I was a girl. She would have nothing of it. I thought she would just go crazy on me whenever I would mention any of that kind of thing. So, like so many things, as you'll find out, I kept it to myself.

My parents had gone through many hard times, before, during, and after I was born, but when it came to shrimping, Mom and Dad were a team. They'd go out on one of their bigger boats for at least a week, and sometimes longer. That's how the bills got paid. They'd go out and catch as much shrimp as they could, take it all to a shrimping dock to sell it, refuel and restock the boat with ice and groceries, and then head back out to sea.

The shrimping season always opened in May—in fact, almost always precisely on my birthday. That meant that my parents would be out shrimping on the bayou when my birthday rolled around, and they wouldn't be around to celebrate it with me. It was sad for me. Sure, we would always celebrate my birthday when they returned, but it just wasn't the same. My birthday went by just like any other day. In the rare year that they were home, they would take me to Biloxi Beach with a couple of their closest friends that we grew up with. We called them "Aunt" and "Uncle" even though they weren't actually blood relations. We were all like family—and still are family today.

Come summer, when we were finally out of school, Shanna, Jesse, and I would be on the boats with my parents. We were extra "picking hands" and could help them out. I learned how to work a salt barrel; we'd put all the catch inside it, and all the fish and other things in the water that weren't shrimp —the "drag"—would float to the top. Then we'd remove all that with a net and separate the shrimp into different sizes. My dad would come and fill up the ice hole and put all the shrimp in. The process would take about 30 to 60 minutes to clean the catch like that. And then we'd do it all over again.

We'd do that all day, and sometimes, depending on the tide or where we were, we'd do it all night, too. We'd only get maybe three or four hours of sleep for several days in a row. It was grueling and exhausting work.

And I completely hated it! It was like torture to me. Of course, I'm a hard worker and something of a perfectionist, so everything I did had to be perfect. The shrimp had to be cleaned meticulously. I took it all so seriously. Later, as a teenager, I couldn't help thinking that there must be something better for me to be doing in my life besides sweating profusely, smelling like rotten shrimp, and being slathered with Skin so Soft to keep the deer flies from eating me alive. In between drag cleaning, I would sleep from being so exhausted. But I have to admit that when we were done working, I absolutely loved sitting on the top deck, listening to the seagulls, feeling the gentle breeze when there was one (which was rare), watching the waves and the shrimp boat move up and down, and listening to music while we were running from one location to another. It was heaven! It felt so free. I enjoyed that a lot— just not the shrimping part.

My dad had discovered shrimping a long time ago. When he was 15 years old, he accepted a job as a deckhand on a 65-foot shrimp boat out of Freeport, Texas. But he hated it. He was seasick most of the time, so it was pretty miserable and exhausting for him. Later, he swore to himself that he would never be on another shrimp boat unless he owned it and was the captain.

A few years later, he became a welder and decided to take on odd jobs to provide for his wife and newborn. But when the welding work slowed and the market plummeted too much to be able to pay the bills, he started building boats. That changed everything. Soon enough, thanks to his boat business and later, shrimping, he was able to build a nice house for the family.

As far back as I can remember, there were always a lot of boats in front of the house. My dad built boats out of steel, then aluminum, and then began building smaller ones with cabin bathrooms and kitchens and all sorts of things. The first shrimp boat he ever built was a 40-foot steel hull boat that he built in our front yard when I was about five years old. My dad's largest boat, Miss Cindy, was a 50x18 steel double rigger with a 671hp GM engine.

We had a very scary incident on Miss Cindy. We were getting her ready for her first sea trial and ventured out to the icehouse for ice and fuel. But once we got there, the engine failed. The water current was so strong that it carried us out to the Intracoastal Waterway, where a river tug was moving barges at full speed. We were terrorized, thinking that it might run into us. The captain of the tug tried to slow it down, but it wasn't enough, and all we could do was brace for impact. It hit us while we hid in the cabin, and the boat bobbed up and down like a cork with a fish attached. We survived uninjured, and the boat didn't sink, but that day, we all thanked God it wasn't any worse.

There was always something about that boat that just didn't sit well with me. Now, storms brew really quickly on the water; it could be beautiful weather one minute and raging seas the next, so, sure enough, Miss Cindy got caught in an unexpected storm. The seas were blustering, the boat was bobbing up and down, and the water rushed over the bow of the boat while my dad tried furiously to navigate her into a smaller bayou for safety. Those kinds of experiences never get forgotten.

But the shrimp boat in the yard intrigued me. One day, late in the afternoon, I wanted to help paint it for some reason, so, despite my parents' warnings, I climbed up the ladder to the boat. I already had a fear of heights by that time, but I couldn't help myself. Seeing what I was doing, my parents yelled to me not to move from where I was, but I ignored them. I looked around, being somewhat nosey, and found the engine hole, which was empty because the engine had been taken out. It had steel bars rising out of it like a tic-tac-toe board for the engine to sit on, and someone had placed a board over it to stop people from falling in, of course. But I moved the board to see what was inside. (No surprise that people called me "Nosy Rosey" from time to time.) I took a step and fell right into the hole. Soon covered in diesel, I screamed like crazy. When my dad heard me, he came and pulled me out and brought me into the house. They threw me in the bathtub and checked to see if I was bleeding or if anything was broken. Nothing was broken, but the fall left a strong impression on me. More to be afraid of, I guess. Later, I found out it may have contributed to my getting a concussion that none of us knew about.

I had begun a longstanding habit of rocking back and forth in my crib back when I was about six months old. Now, much research shows that it's quite common for children to rock their bodies and roll their heads at nighttime, in their sleep, and during naps. It is known to be rhythmic, and it is considered comforting and soothing for a child. But when I was about five years old, the rocking turned into headbanging. My parents didn't understand it and were very concerned about me, so they took me to a pediatrician. He looked me over, asked me some questions, and told my parents them it was very common and that he didn't think it was a problem. He added that if I was actually harming myself, then I would naturally stop doing it.

Well, that never happened. The banging got worse and began to interrupt my daily functioning. If I was bored, stressed, frustrated, or just overloaded with sensory input, if I couldn't properly communicate what I was feeling, I would start banging my head as a way of releasing what I was feeling. As if that wasn't enough, I would bang my head to music and find songs that would match the emotion I was feeling.

Later, when I was in my 40s, I found out that I showed signs of a concussion. Most likely, it was a result of the headbanging and, oh yeah, the fall into the engine hole. Or maybe it was the go-cart accident I had at 15, when I hit a pine tree in the front yard head-on.

The headbanging didn't fully come to a stop until I was 21, when I moved to Alabama to attend college, joined a sorority, met my best friends, and the love of my life. To this day, I still rock from time to time. It's an automatic response to things that are emotionally charged or when I'm triggered or just maxed out from the energy of others. But the headbanging ended long ago.

It took me a lot of years to realize that I had been an unusually sensitive kid growing up. It was just the kind of thing our family didn't talk about, so I never really processed it fully. Like my mom, I could see and sense things. People noticed and told me I was "different." Even at the age of three, I was often in my own little world. I could see dead people, hear voices, feel the presence of energy, see angels, and sometimes monsters. I sensed all sorts of energies around everyone that I came in contact with. I physically felt what people were feeling, I'd emotionally experience it, and even visually see it in my mind's eye and with my physical eyes, too, sometimes. A lot of it scared me. But, as a result, I learned to "read" people very early on in life. I was like a sponge, absorbing all of it and then keeping it as my own as if it were my responsibility to take care of it.

Still, I never told people what I saw or felt. I just kept it all in and tucked it away, allowing my body, mind, spirit, and soul to keep the scores. That way, I didn't have to deal with it.

One incident is especially telling. My Maw Maw had a rocking horse in the back room of her house—in fact, it had been my mother's bedroom when she was a girl—and I would just rock on it to my heart's content. The paneling in that room had a pattern that looked like wood knots. One day, I started seeing monsters coming out of the paneling, and I started screaming. I was on the rocking horse, and I was rocking so hard I thought I had broken the springs on it. I was deathly afraid of what was coming out of the paneling. So I cried a lot.

I also cried when I saw other people being hurt. I hated to be picked on—and I sure did get picked on—but then I reasoned that at least I was saving someone else from being the target of someone's meanness. People told me I wore my heart on my sleeve and called me a worrywart. (They called me "Fat Potato," too, from time to time, but that's another story.) I worried about everyone and everything. From that point on, I had a lot of fear and anxiety from what I was seeing of the non-physical world.

It was overwhelming at times. There were so many feelings to feel, I didn't know what I was feeling. I could sense other people's negative emotions so deeply—their anger, criticism, defeat, and distress. Even though I was so young, loud noises, sudden changes, new situations, and the quicksand of other people's emotional distress started to foster fear in me.

So, even though I did a lot of kid things with my siblings and my cousins, I never quite felt like I fit in. I was always internal, in my inner thoughts and feelings. There was just so much going on inside me, I would much rather be alone. It was one of the best ways I had to decompress and feel less overwhelmed in life. Being around other people—of any age—drained the life out of me.

My sister, Shanna, had her challenges, too. From the time she was born, she has had to struggle with the symptoms of asthma. There were many times when, because the mucus had built up so badly in her lungs, we would have to pat her hard with the palms of our hands—almost beat her, it felt like—on her side and waist and where her ribs were to keep the mucus from collecting. When we were done, I'd just lie there with her, trying to comfort her. It was exhausting and traumatizing.

Then, just five days before her fourth birthday, my baby sister almost died from asthma. Shanna was having terrible trouble breathing, so she was taken to her pediatrician, who had her admitted to the hospital. But when both of her lungs collapsed, they had to rush her to New Orleans to a facility that could help her. They told us they didn't know if she was going to survive or not.

When they finally brought her home, she looked as frail as a porcelain baby doll with long golden-blonde hair. My heart was broken for her, knowing that she almost died had been devastating. I was nine years old, and I had just watched her fight for her life. It was a lot for me to take in at nine years old. It gave me a lot to ponder.

It was a very hard time for all of us. My dad was working and was tired a lot, my mom was busy taking care of us kids, and Shanna refused to sleep in her bed and lie down. The three of us took turns consoling and rocking her because she wanted to be held all the time. Mom said I would often stay up with her and rock her at night so they could get some rest.

Then, when I was thirteen, my dad's brother died of leukemia. My uncle and I were very close, so it was a very emotional time for me. Making it even harder on me was the fact that I had written a letter to him that I wanted to put in his coffin at the burial, but my parents wouldn't allow me to go. In those days, children didn't go to funerals—much less talk about death or about nearly dying. (My Paw Paw fell over in his wheelchair while fishing one day, and thankfully my brother was there and saved him. It was upsetting to me. But no one ever talked about it.)

Since my parents were away at the funeral, Shanna, Jesse, and I had been staying at my Maw Maw and Paw Paw's house. We needed to go to the local store to pick up some bread or milk, so we all started to climb into my grandparents' van. But we didn't know that their German Shephard, Missy, was in the van at the time.

Missy was a rescue dog that my Maw Maw had taken in. We didn't know much about her background or behavior, but she had spent a lot of time with us kids, so she seemed safe enough. To us, she was just another member of the family.

But maybe she got territorial about the van. As we got ready to go to the store, I took the responsible role, as usual, and rallied up my siblings to get in the van to leave. None of us knew that the dog had found her way inside the van. But, as we approached the vehicle and started climbing in, the dog lashed out suddenly. My sister was in my arms, and I instinctually moved her in front me to lift her into the van. Then, before we even knew what was happening, Missy jumped forward, sunk her teeth into Shanna's calf, and wouldn't let go. With Shanna's entire leg in her mouth, she shook from head to toe, like she was ready for the kill, like she was in a trance. We screamed and screamed, trying to get the dog to let go. Her bite had separated the muscle on my sister's leg and she ended up needing extensive surgery to try to repair it. The scars on her legs are still visible to this day.

I felt incredibly responsible for Shanna's pain that day. No one else really blamed me, but I blamed myself for the longest time, thinking I should have put myself in front of her, not the other way around. I should have made sure the dog attacked *me* instead of her.

I replayed the scenarios like that over and over in my mind all throughout my childhood. I thought about all the things I could have and should have done differently for my sister, my brother, and other people I knew. Any time my brother got into trouble or hurt himself— and there were a lot of those times—I'd think I should have been able to prevent it. Again, I put myself into a parental role, thinking I was responsible for the lives and well-being of Shanna and Jesse. I dwelled on those stories and hung onto my regrets and self-punishment. I didn't know how to let things go. Making matters worse, I kept it all to myself and never told anyone what I was experiencing.

And I still have my uncle's letter.

CHAPTER 2

THE BULLY

People who repeatedly attack your confidence and
self-esteem are quite aware of your potential, even if you are not.
~Wayne Gerard Trotman

It wasn't until 2014 that Maw Maw told me I had been bitten by a tick when I was about seven years old—and I started to think that maybe there was a reason after all for all of the crazy, painful twists and turns my life took since I was a kid. She said that Paw Paw had tried to use a burning match to "back" the tick out, but we really didn't know if it worked or not. In fact, these days, they say that's the worst thing you can do to clean out a tick bite. Personally, I don't have a memory of the incident, but it does make me wonder if it exacerbated the very real emotional storm that was brewing inside of me—or if it was the true beginning of the mysterious and elusive illness that would ravage my body, mind, spirit, and soul for many years to come.

I might never know for sure.

About the time I was entering first grade, I started getting regular bouts of diarrhea and constipation, headaches, and early signs of short-term memory loss. One or the other would just appear out of nowhere and take me out. No one seemed to understand what was causing any of it. The doctors just told my parents that it was because I was nervous and a worrier and they gave me prescriptions for amoxicillin, a penicillin antibiotic, just in case something was wrong. I liked it because it tasted like bubble gum.

My parents thought I was having emotional difficulties adjusting to the new grade, but it wasn't that. I was having trouble with my studies. At first, it wasn't a big deal to me because my first-grade teacher was kind and compassionate and helped me with my lessons. Math and numbers gave me fits. While I loved to read, and I could read very quickly, I had to re-read something over and over again to comprehend it. Turns out, I needed a tutor to help me. I compared myself to the other students who did not have to work so hard. I envied them, wanting to be smart like them. Embarrassed about it, I started to become very private, not wanting anyone to know my business. If they did not know anything, I figured, then they would leave me alone.

But my teacher was amazing that year. She was able to lift me when I was down. In fact, she seemed to be able to breathe life into all of us, treating us like we were her own children. She seemed to want us to succeed.

In second grade, my academic difficulties started giving me more trouble, and my new teacher made matters even worse. She scared me to death. I started to hate school, and I cried a lot. Many of the teachers at school liked to use shame as a tool and a weapon. They made a practice of calling out our test scores so that everyone in class would know how we did—good or bad. To those of us who weren't high performers, it was humiliating. No one wanted to be the kid with the F and get embarrassed in class, with everyone thinking that you were either stupid or you didn't study. You'd have to explain why you made an F on your test. I also hated getting those "Deficiency Slips"—and I got many of them—a few weeks before report cards came out in school. I'd get terribly fearful about getting in trouble when it came time to showing my parents. I decided I was not going to keeping going down that road, so I started studying extra hard.

Even though I was in the second grade, I took it upon myself to ask my first-grade teacher for help, since she had been helpful the year before and I knew she wouldn't judge me. I thought, *What better person to help with the things I struggle the most with—math, reading, and writing?* But when my second-grade teacher found out about it, she made a point of thoroughly embarrassing me in front of the classroom, slapping a ruler on the top of my desk during a math lesson. In front of the whole class, she told me that she thought I would never amount to anything. Emotionally, I started to withdraw, since the outer world just didn't seem to be a kind place.

Four years later, when I was in sixth grade, I attended an event for one of my siblings, and I noticed that my former second-grade teacher was there, too. I decided to do the civilized thing and go up to her and say hello. Part of me still wanted to show her that I was not at all the terrible things she said I would be. So, I told her that I had made the honor roll, and she laughed in some weird way.

"I don't believe you are "honor roll" material, Michelle," she said. "Your teacher probably just gave you the grades."

I felt shocked, hurt, rejected, and completely heartbroken. With those two sentences, my world came crashing down once again. I felt defeated as I noticed that nothing had really changed after all. She did not care, anyway. I just retreated inside even more.

Third grade was no better. My anxiety was getting worse. My parents had regular meetings with the teacher to try to figure out what to do to get me back on track and help me out emotionally. The teacher was fairly condescending and judgmental and told them she thought I should repeat the third grade. She thought I wasn't fourth-grade material, she said. But I did move on to the fourth grade, thanks to the principal and my dad.

But my anxiety started getting even worse. I started to worry about the new school I would be entering in fifth grade. It was a much larger school than the elementary school I'd been attending, and the thought of it overwhelmed to me. Looking back, my apprehension might also have been my intuition—warning me of the torment that would follow me for the rest of my school days.

I started getting severe migraines. At first, my parents and I thought the lights in the classroom were causing them, but then my parents thought I should get my eyes checked. Sure enough, I needed glasses to read. We were initially relieved that there was a simple solution, and I thought it was cool to wear glasses for a while. But then kids at school started calling me "Four eyes." I wasn't going to have that, so I refused to wear them at school. I only wore them when at home to study.

On a lighter note, I started to take a liking to softball that summer. I joined a softball league and met some new friends—people who I'm still close with today. The game turned out to be a great way to have fun and release anger and frustration. I could hit the ball as hard as I wanted to, and it felt really good.

In fifth grade, I continued to struggle with my classes, especially math, reading, and writing. Nobody understood or recognized or even heard about dyslexia back then, but I had it, and it made learning very difficult for me. On top of my academic struggles, I also had to manage it emotionally. In schools back then, students with learning problems were taken out of the regular classroom for most of the day and placed in special education classes. Of course, the other kids would end up picking on the Special Ed kids, call them by disturbing names, and just be plain mean to them. I didn't want that to happen to me. Ready to do what it took to avoid getting placed in Special Ed, I forced myself to work hard at my studies to make sure I got passing grades. While some teachers tried to accuse me of being lazy or not working hard enough, it was the opposite. I often stayed up late in my room studying until my mom came in and found me buried in my books. She'd force me to turn off the lights and go to bed. "But I just don't understand the material well enough yet!" I'd argue. It went on this way all through high school. I couldn't remember what I was studying very well, so I was always in the books. I couldn't afford sleep; I just had to keep studying because I just couldn't remember or even recall the material.

I wasn't exactly the cool kid or in the "in crowd" at school. So, I was very excited and felt a certain amount of acceptance when I received an invitation to a birthday slumber party in middle school. It was a great party. I had lots of fun—until I woke up the next morning with people gathered all around me, some staring and some laughing at me.

I had been banging my head in my sleep. I woke up that way. Nobody'd seen it before, and they wanted to get a good look at this crazy person. I was horribly embarrassed by it all. I tried to brush it off, but the tears started coming and wouldn't stop. Finally, my mom came to take me home. By Monday, the entire school had heard about what happened to the weird girl who was banging her head at a slumber party. So I pulled inward even more.

That year, I started to get depressed. And while my life hadn't been easy up until then, it took a steep nosedive.

That's when the bullying started.

She was a tall, big girl, and a grade ahead of me. She taunted me with verbal attacks, called me names, stole my snack money, broke my pencils, threatened to beat me up, and filled my backpack with water. She'd wait for me on the playground, so she could confront me and force me to buy something for her with my own snack money. She threatened to beat me up if I didn't do what she said. I guess I didn't make it hard for her because I just didn't like confrontation. I gave in for the sake of peace. As time went on, I felt less and less of a person—I was always afraid, watching over my shoulder for what might soon bring me more suffering.

This bully always had a little crowd around her—her followers. They just stood by laughing and joining in her so-called games, tormenting me. Even if she wasn't there herself, somebody in her circle would be nearby, watching or taunting me on her behalf.

Sometimes she'd try to make up for what she did by offering me all sorts of candy on the bus ride home. But then she'd make a point of sitting behind or across from me on the bus, and I hated that. It took the school a long time to finally make her sit far away from me. Eventually, I made a habit of sitting behind the bus driver so I didn't have to deal with anyone anymore. I felt safer there.

She never let up; I was the only one she harassed. I was a small-framed, thoughtful, introverted, young woman, and of course, I hated confrontation, so it was torture for me on many fronts. I don't know why she picked me to torment, but I was probably the perfect target, the perfect victim, because I'd take it, and she would get away with her antics. Worse, for some reason, I didn't want her to get in trouble, so, for a long time, I even defended her to the authorities, thinking maybe I did something to her that I was unaware of at the time.

I hated school and started to feel very depressed. I was always sick with a stomachache and tried to find every excuse I could to not have to go. Still, she taunted me every day and got away with almost everything she did. She had a way about her—she pretended to be friendly, and then she would strike with insults. She was controlling, sneaky, aggressive, and fake—all at the same time. My parents went to school numerous times to report what was happening, but nothing meaningful was ever done. Every time the girl was called to the principal's office, she would deny everything and play the victim by crying and trying to look pitiful. Then, sometime soon after that, she would turn around and retaliate against me in some way. Nobody did anything meaningful to stop her. The torture continued.

One day, my parents bought me an awesome pink bat because they knew I loved playing softball. It was my favorite sport, and I was good at it. Some of us played softball at lunch recess until the bell rang for us to line up to go back inside. But one day, my tormenter walked over to me and asked to see my bat. Of course, I knew she was up to no good, but she was a big girl, and I didn't want trouble. I figured that if I just gave her what she wanted; she would leave me alone. No surprise, she grabbed my bat and threw it as far as she possibly could, over the fence, and into a ditch. Then she turned around, looked at me, and laughed. When I told the teacher about it, all she made her do was tell me she was sorry. Once again, my parents went to the school to get the issue attended to. But again, the school did little more than lip service.

I became a nervous wreck and retreated into myself more. I was scared to even go to the bathroom out of fear that she'd corner me, threaten me, or worse. At recess, I tried to find ways to stay inside and avoid becoming a target once we were outside. I'd ask the teacher—of whatever grade I was in—if they needed help with something to give me an excuse to stay inside. But that backfired when I started getting labeled the "teacher's pet" each year. She had threatened that she'd beat me up if I told the teachers about what she did. I was just trying to stay safe and avoid the evil that was lurking in my path if I ventured outside.

After this continued for a while, I started having a hard time trusting anyone. I had been dealing with too many people whose words and actions didn't match up, and it had an effect on me. Who could I trust? Who was on my side? Who was out to get me? I wasn't sure.

My torturer continued to bully me in sixth grade, and it started to affect all aspects of my life. My parents went back to the school again to complain and then tried to reach out to the school board, but still, nothing happened. Worse, the bully's mother called and threatened to sue us for picking on her daughter, claiming that *I* was the one harassing *her*.

The strange thing was that I was the one feeling bad about all of it. I was ashamed, and I felt bad for her, even felt sorry for her. I wondered what I had done wrong to deserve it. I asked myself again and again, what I did do to deserve the treatment she gave me. What did I do to make her angry? And sometimes I justified it all, thinking that if she was picking on me, she was leaving someone else alone. I was helping save someone else from getting hurt.

I was still suffering from the unpredictability of my ping-ponging digestion—back and forth between diarrhea and constipation. When it got really bad, my mom took me to the doctor, who said, "She just worries about *everything!*" and they just chalked it all up to that once again. Between being plagued by my stomach distress, learning challenges, memory problems, and the fear and anxiety about what the bully would do to me next, my whole existence seemed to be an uphill battle.

Thankfully, I was doing well in sixth grade academically. After all my hard work, I made the honor roll, and, for the first time, I felt proud of myself. It looked like my determination was paying off. My teacher was a kind and gentle person, too. But when my parents met with her at their annual parent-teacher conference, she told them she thought that I lacked confidence and that I didn't believe in myself. After hearing that, despite the accomplishment of making the honor roll, I fell back into self-criticism and doubt.

Music had become an outlet for me. It was one way that I could escape from the stresses of my world and even feel good about myself for a little while. In fifth grade, my parents let me join the school band, which became one of the few safe spaces for me. I chose the saxophone as my instrument. My cousin had loaned me a second-hand sax that I could use, and I was off and running. Just before the school's Christmas concert, I had made "first chair"—I was chosen as the designated leader of the section, the one closest to the audience. It was a big deal! Then, one Friday night, my parents went out to go shrimping and returned Sunday night, so my dad could go to his job the next day. They must have done well selling their shrimp at the shrimp dock on Monday because they surprised me with a brand-new saxophone that night. I was elated! I had enough time before the Christmas concert to practice with my new instrument and get it just right. I was in heaven.

When I entered seventh grade, the bully had moved onto junior high, so she wasn't at the same school—and couldn't bully me. But in eighth grade, there she was again, in my face, attacking me with gossiping, snickering, and making up rumors about me. By that time, I started having boyfriends, so I got a little protection and a little feeling of safety from them.

While all this was going on, when I was 14, I decided I wanted to enter a local beauty pageant, and my parents gave me permission. I loved it. I loved playing with hair, makeup, and fashion. There was a ton of prep work to do, too, including mock interviews, walking practice, learning to tilt your head this way and position your hands another way, smile this way, use your eyes to speak, and more. The list of what to do just goes on and on. And if it wasn't good enough, I'd do it again until I got it right.

It didn't take long for me to get obsessed about it all. I won most of the pageants I entered, starting at age 14. At my first pageant, I wore a beautiful pink-sequined, ruffled top with a full skirt with a petticoat underneath to give it the full effect. My hair and makeup were perfect. I walked across the stage with a beautiful smile, gracefully and confidently, and the members of my family who were in the audience yelled out with their approval and support. It was a small win, a temporary parting of the clouds within a brewing, dark storm. I became a pro at wearing a mask. The pageants allowed me to become someone else for a while.

Not surprisingly, I had a seesaw, love/hate relationship with myself around the pageants. When I was down to a certain size or felt I looked a certain way or had a certain tan, it all made me feel good about myself for a while. But I sensed that it wasn't enough. While I might have loved what I saw on the outside for a moment, my insides were just kind of rotting away. One minute I loved it, the next minute I'd hate everything about it. Most of the time, when I looked in the mirror, I hated everything I saw, magnified every flaw. I exercised like crazy and tried every diet imaginable so I could remain a certain size. After a while, I became an emotional eater and used food as a comforter, only to hate myself for eating. That meant that, despite my traumatic experiences with diarrhea, I'd take laxatives from time to time to avoid gaining weight. I didn't want to vomit, so I chose laxatives to give myself diarrhea.

CHAPTER 3

THE YO-YO

Our faith is built in the dark, in the valleys, and
during the back-breaking battles in life.
~Dana Arcuri

Thankfully, ninth grade was somewhat peaceful for me. My bully had entered high school, and I was left in peace for a little while. I got more active in band, became one of two drum majors, joined a youth group, started to enjoy softball a little more, and started dating my new love. Junior high was actually looking up.

My boyfriend was, in many ways, my protector. He was a great guy, and I sometimes thought he was "the one" and that we would ride off into the sunset together and live happily ever. We dated all through high school, and a few years off and on after that, before the relationship shattered into a million pieces. He endured more than he probably bargained for. I made some poor choices and decisions that caused us to separate and felt a lot of guilt and shame because of it.

I was still wrestling with illness in high school. To my surprise, I got diagnosed with mononucleosis in my junior year of high school, which was extremely painful. The kids teased me about it because it was called "the kissing disease." It meant that I had to suffer through exhausting fatigue, swollen lymph nodes, fever, and body aches, which I had assumed was just a fallout of being involved in so many different activities in school. I was also putting tremendous pressure on myself to achieve, and I pushed myself to try extra hard just to stay on top of my studies. I didn't want to be embarrassed by poor grades. Besides, my boyfriend was very smart—he got straight A's and scored high on the ACT's—and I worried that I wasn't measuring up in his mind or mine. I had taken the ACT once, and I had been so embarrassed by my score, that I considered myself dumb. So I worked at everything that much harder.

I had tried out for the marching band in eighth grade, and the band director was kind enough to tell me I had "leadership qualities" and to encourage me to try out as a drum major once I got to ninth grade. I had no idea what he meant, but I followed his advice. So, in ninth grade, I tried out and made it.

In fact, there were just two drum majors in ninth grade: my boyfriend and me. It took a lot of hard work, dedication, and practice, and I struggled to remember the routines, but I did enjoy it somewhat. But then I would get overwhelmed, and panic would set in. I didn't share with anyone what I was feeling because I was embarrassed, and it seemed to come easy to everyone else.

At 16, I entered high school and found that hell was waiting for me once again. My bully resumed her verbal attacks, but, by that time, I had several people who had my back, so I felt somewhat protected and safe from her. I did what I could, basically stood up for myself as much as I could. After all, I had a boyfriend, I was hanging out with the band, and softball consumed most of my time, too, so she couldn't get to me quite like she had before. And I had a teacher I trusted who let me know I could go to for help if something happened. Thankfully, I was learning to let in a tiny bit of support.

Then—finally—I stood up for myself in front of my tormentor, and we never spoke after that day. Praise God! She was gone!

But I was still on a pretty severe emotional roller-coaster ride. My chronic digestion problems, difficulties with learning, challenges with the bully, and even my involvement with the beauty pageants created a maelstrom of pain in my psyche. I felt like a complete misfit, consumed with other people's judgments and expectations.

I was plagued with feelings of being abandoned, unloved, and not being good enough because I had been internalizing everything. I refused to discuss any of it with anyone due to a fear of the reactions I thought I would receive. What would someone think of me? Many were clueless anyway, so what was the point? I regularly retreated from the world since it was a safe, although very lonely place for me.

My emotions were up and down like a yo-yo, and it started to affect my eating, too. I wouldn't eat all day, but then I'd eat everything in sight in the evenings. The pageants I entered, of course, instilled a pressure to stay skinny and make that a priority. But with everything else going on, it was virtually impossible for me to do. My body wasn't very cooperative. I was exhausted.

I also had no idea who I was supposed to be or who I wanted to be. At one point, I thought I might want to go to a convent and become a nun. Then I could be alone in solitude and give my life to Jesus because it wasn't working out so well for me in the real world with these so-called humans. The depression had really set in by this time. I thought I was fat and ugly every time I looked into the mirror. I saw every flaw I could possibly find on my body. I had no self-worth, no self-esteem, no confidence, and no love for myself. I became filled with anger, bitterness, doubt, and resentment, and I could get pissed without any reason and give someone the silent treatment without even thinking about it. I had a huge wall around me and would not let anyone get too close.

Being a private person, I would get angry when it seemed that people were trying to probe into my life, my feelings, or my conditions. I had the attitude that if I wanted you to know, then I would tell you—otherwise, mind your own business. My trust issues were deepening, as I was on the receiving end of so much judgment, betrayal, and hurt. It would always seem to turn out that the one time I trusted someone, I'd get betrayed, or the one person I "trusted" would blab a secret or two of mine to the entire world or judge me for it. Once again, I felt ashamed and humiliated, and I layered a tremendous amount of guilt on top of that.

I didn't have many girlfriends through high school—just a couple of friends I hung out with. I liked to be nice and talk to everyone, but I didn't trust hardly anyone enough to allow them into my inner world. I managed to always be friendly, but I was sure to keep people at a distance.

And I continued to keep my deepest feelings to myself. I didn't even share most of what I was feeling with my boyfriend. Unfortunately, he ended up catching the backlash of it all—I could become just an awful person when I was triggered. It was not uncommon for me just to be pissed off and shut down and give him the total silent treatment. Then he would try to find out what was going on, which only caused me to fill up with more rage, ending in some sort of outburst. Then that would turn into a fight for no reason. I never had an answer for him—it was all too overwhelming and intense for me—and it caused tension between us.

My relationship with my mom continued to be strained and argumentative as I grew older, too. It got even worse in high school when she kept insisting on setting up all sorts of rules and limitations for my life. Restrictions that no one else I knew had to conform to. Her heavy hand on me was very hard for me to deal with and only added to my feelings of being isolated, alone, and overwhelmed.

My 17th birthday started out just fine. I received a dozen beautiful red roses from my parents and had a decent day at school. At the end of the school day, my dad picked me up to drive me home, but as we turned onto our street, we were in shock over what we saw. We saw a man lying on the ground, screaming for help, his chest all bloody, from a robbery that had happened minutes before we arrived on the scene. He and another man had been waiting to buy crawfish from local fishermen before the robbery. The other man had also been shot and had been taken to a local convenient store to call for help. Apparently, it was a botched robbery and attempted murder. Other people began to arrive, so my dad and I went to store parking lot to get out of the way and to check on the guy who went to call for help. Cops and ambulances arrived. People started gathering to be nosey; after all, our small town was a gossip hub. Cops began taking statements, so we left. Mom said that when we arrived home, I was a complete basket case. Praise God, no one perished that day; they were only injured from the spray of bullets. But it was awful.

I refused to go to school the following day because some of the kids I went to school with were relatives of the accused, and I didn't want my presence to cause repercussions on my family and me just for being at the scene. In our town, everybody knew everybody—and word travels quickly. I did go to school the following day, but I made sure to stay in hiding from the shock and paranoia. The incident filled me with so much fear and anxiety that I had nightmares for weeks afterward.

My digestive issues were still awful all through high school. In my senior year, our softball team won the state championship, but before the game started, I got terribly sick with the worst diarrhea I'd ever had. The coach kept sending people over to me to tell me to get my ass back on the field. But I wasn't completely a no-show. I hit a triple that day, which advanced us to the championship.

After I graduated high school, I got to compete in the Miss USA/ Louisiana swimsuit and evening gown competition, which was a big deal. The winner becomes a contestant in the Miss U.S.A. pageant we all see on TV. I was a perfectionist and compared myself to everyone else, never measuring up, of course. So many of them were tall, beautiful, and slender—I mean, they were tiny! On the other hand, I was 5' 3" and about 132 pounds—too big to get anywhere in the modeling world at that time. Besides, I was "carrying" a lot—including body-shame and jealousy. Yet when I look at the pictures I have from those days, pictures of me walking across the stage during that competition, I can't help but wonder what in the world I was thinking—being so harsh and critical of myself! I was gorgeous, even beaming and confident! But on the inside, the young woman on that stage was a lost soul, searching for love and acceptance, not realizing she already had it in her.

Realistically, I was very much out of my league. One girl arrived at the event with her own personal makeup artists and hairstylists and had brought a trunk full of brand-new outfits. She had to take time to choose which one she was going to wear for the event. How was I supposed to compete with that? My family, on the other hand, didn't have a lot of money to spend on such things. My parents worked hard just to provide me with one new evening gown. For my swimsuit, we went all the way to Baton Rouge, Louisiana, to go do my prep. They had a trunk with all the latest fashions that we could look through. When I was reminiscing with my mom about it later, she put it this way:

"Well, it sure was hard for us to get $120 to buy you a bathing suit so that you would be in style and match the look of the other girls on stage. That was $120 that we didn't have—but we knew it was important to you, so we found a way."

Some family and friends contributed small donations to help cover the fees and other miscellaneous costs.

I felt like I didn't belong; I thought I wasn't classy enough. And, well, it was a high-class operation, and I couldn't help but feel out of my league. All the other girls had a whole team of people helping them with every aspect of the competition. My "team" consisted of just me and my mom. I felt like about one inch tall compared to them. Even more, I can't tell you how many times I had to wash my face and reapply fresh makeup. My face was raw and irritated by the time the weekend was over.

That was my last pageant. A local director who had been training me for Miss Louisiana/USA asked me to judge occasionally, so I did that for a while. It was difficult to do because I hated having to put negative comments on people's score sheets. One of the categories was "Beauty," and I had to rate them from 1 to 10. I wanted to give them all a 10. After all, when I was competing, some of the judges weren't so nice when they scored me, and I knew it made me feel even worse about myself.

Religion has been a part of my life since I was a little girl, and it continued to be meaningful for me as I became an adult. As a girl, my family had been the kind of family that attends the local Catholic church every Sunday. I was baptized as a baby and made my first communion when I was in the second grade. My Maw Maw and Paw Paw gave me the most beautiful rosary for my communion, which I still treasure today. Catechism every Wednesday was the beginning of my religious education of growing in the love and knowledge of God. I had my confirmation in the 11th grade with our bishop.

In junior high and high school, I joined the Diocese Youth Group. We helped elderly people in the community travel to conferences, painted some of their houses, and helped with home maintenance, among other things. The sheer joy that some of them expressed to us was incredibly rewarding. I made some new friends in the group, and I thoroughly enjoyed it. I felt like I belonged to something and that I was making a difference.

Then I met Sister Fatima. She was sent as a replacement because we no longer had a resident priest. She was an amazing role model for me, and her dedication to Jesus spoke to my heart. I loved going to the rectory just to be in her presence and just to talk. She always said there was some sort of "presence" about me, so I decided to do the readings on Sunday. Sister Fatima remained a part of my life and was even present on my wedding day. But once she left our community and I moved away, we lost touch.

I also met Sister Mary Elaine during a summer Bible Camp. Sister Mary Elaine had a very gentle disposition and encouraged me to visit her and the Marianites of Holy Cross, who are known for their love, compassion, gratitude, and listening. For a brief moment, I considered becoming a nun. I already lived a life of isolation, pretending all was well in front of everyone. I begin to think maybe that's the life that was right for me. But ultimately, I never made that trip because it wasn't my calling.

I had no intention of going to college because I struggled and didn't think I was smart enough to attend. No matter how much I studied, I struggled with just remembering everything I had read. But I knew I wanted to be of service and pour my heart into helping others, so I enrolled in Young Memorial Technical College to become a Certified Nursing Assistant in hopes of becoming an LPN and maybe even an RN someday.

It wasn't easy for me. I struggled terribly with biology and chemistry, studied as hard as I could, and still barely passed. I joined a study group, and we'd study together all night. Yet while everyone else would make A's, I would make C's, D's, and F's. Once again, I felt like a loser.

After completing my CNA, I took a job at a local nursing home on their Skill Unit as a certified nursing assistant. I decided to skip the LPN and, instead, applied to Nicholls State University to begin working towards being an RN.

The unit I worked on at the nursing home was basically for people who were dying. The floor reeked with the smell of death. The conditions there made me vow that I would never allow my parents to go to that kind of place when they got older and couldn't care for themselves any longer.

But it was my job to care for and love on the patients as they left the physical world and went to Jesus. Most of them had no family, and my heart hurt for them. Most of them wanted me to hold them or hold their hands. I was their comfort; I helped to release them of their pain and suffering with laying of hands before they left this world.

In the fall of 1994, I entered Nicholls State University in Thibodaux, Louisiana as a nursing student. It was at Nicholls that I started to realize that I could take away people's pain; in fact, I finally acknowledged that I had been doing just that since the age of three even though I hadn't realized it. God had given me special gifts, and He showed them to me and helped me learn about them during that time. I could feel people's pain, and I was able to calm them. I was not afraid, and I didn't want them to be afraid either, for I felt that they were not alone. I was there for them and with them. But I didn't yet know how to separate their pain from my own. I didn't really know what to do with their suffering, so I just stored their pain along with my own. I didn't know how to process or release any of it yet. I just piled everything onto my internal burdens, which I wasn't handling too well, either.

I moved on. I worked as a sitter for the elderly for a while. Then I moved over to the physical therapy ward, working nights at the local hospital as a CNA for a change of pace.

After my boyfriend and I officially broke up—he was already seeing someone else according to a long phone conversation I had with someone close to him—I couldn't take living in my small town any longer. I wanted to get as far away as possible. Hoping to get into clinicals—supervised interactions with patients—my friend from NSU and I decided to transfer to the University of South Alabama and apply for clinicals there. I still needed additional credits, so I would need to take some classes once I got there.

On January 1, 1996, my friend told me she had changed her mind about going to USA. So, I began the journey all by myself. I moved into my dormitory on the campus of the University of South Alabama in Mobile, Alabama, to attend their nursing program, but quickly changed my major to Elementary Education. Looking back, I think that I moved more out of a need to run away from my feelings and problems than anything else. My life had been falling apart; I had made too many poor choices, and I was carrying the heavy guilt of knowing that I had deeply hurt the one person I loved at the time. I felt so damaged and broken and hurt, I needed to lash out and hurt him in order to help me feel better. Of course, it backfired. It destroyed the relationship beyond repair. We stopped talking and moved on.

The move to Alabama was the first time I had been out on my own in life, not tethered to my parents. I had no idea what it would be like to be on my own—all of three and a half hours away from home. Of course, I brought my emotional baggage with me. I was wracked with guilt and suffered from intense anxiety and depression, somehow nursing a deep sense of sadness as well.

But the move was almost more than I could take. The combination of the feelings I was holding about the past, my deep grief, the stress of moving away from home, and the effects of a moldy dorm room sent my body and my health into a downward spiral. I ended up spending a lot of time in the campus infirmary, sick with sinus infections and bronchitis, for which they usually gave me antibiotics. My eating was pretty bad, too, as I consumed all sorts of highly processed and fast food—it was just easier to manage with all of the studying I needed to do.

I weighed 122 pounds when I moved to Alabama, so watching what I ate was not literally a necessity, but at the same time, it was. I needed to stay "skinny." I did not want to be fat. I had all the programming from my years in the pageants, and my weight was inextricably linked to embarrassment, shame, guilt, and low self-worth. Additional weight meant saying goodbye to self-love and self-worth.

In fact, food started to become my "go-to" solution to deal with my emotional issues since I was no longer banging my head. I started binge-eating and using laxatives to get rid of what I ate so I wouldn't gain. Binging helped me numb the pain of the past, too, stuffing my feelings down. I reverted back to endless cycles of diets, diet pills, and exercise to shed any extra pounds.

Not surprisingly, I had no energy, and I spent many nights in bed instead of going out with new friends who were becoming my new family. I was living in an unfamiliar state, trying to pick up the pieces of my life, pieces that kept falling out of my hands like a failed juggling act.

I thank God for answered prayers because He brought the love of my life, Steve Potter, into my life.

The day I arrived at school in Mobile, I spent a lot of time unpacking my things. As the day settled down and I began watching a Danielle Steele movie on Lifetime TV, I heard someone knocking on my door. Looking through the peephole, I saw my neighbor Bowdie and his friend, who everyone called "Canada" because that's where she came from. Canada entered my room as if she owned it, sat on my bed, and introduced herself. I thought, *What in the world? Who is this?*

She said, "Can I use your washroom?" I had no idea what a "washroom" was at the time—I thought it was a laundry room! Canada has become a friend for life, and we still laugh about that night today.

Later that day, they invited me to a card game downstairs at their best friend's dorm room. Guess who? Yep, it was the very first time I met the life of the party, Steve Potter.

I will never forget that moment. As soon as I walked into the room, Steve turned to me and said, "Who the hell are you?" My thoughts were, *Who the hell are you?* And: *What an idiot!* We still laugh about our meeting to this today.

The four of us sat down and played several games of Spades, and it just so happened that I had to be Steve's card partner. I thought, *Lucky me! I can't stand the dude already!* I had no idea how to play Spades, so it created a lot to laugh about. As we argued and fought playfully most of the night, I never would have guessed that I would marry this man one day and that he would be the father of my children. That night created a lifetime of love and friendships. For the very first time in my life, I felt like I belonged somewhere.

Then I decided to do an informal rush. Several of the girls I met on campus belonged to sororities and suggested I should, too. I thought it would be a great idea to get involved and meet new people. I met Allison, from Chi Omega, who became my big sister in the sorority, and I instantly felt like I belonged there. But whether I would receive a bid was another question.

When the day arrived for bids to be offered, I could not believe that some of my new sisters showed up at my dorm with balloons. My bid was one of the greatest days of my life—I was going to be a part of something bigger than myself, and I loved that. Better yet, I was selected as Pledge Class President.

One of my favorite events was our yearly Songfest, where Greek life organizations would compete for the trophy and their earnings would benefit the charity of their choice. Any leftovers would benefit our charities, too. It was a lot of fun, upbeat, and energetic, and, on top of everything else, it was a great way for me to come out of isolation.

What stood out for me most about the experience was our beautiful Symphony, which reflected a fresh new start to life—something near and dear to my heart:

Chi Omega Symphony

To live constantly above snobbery of word or deed; to place scholarship before social obligations and character before appearances; to be in the best sense, democratic rather than "exclusive", and lovable rather than "popular"; to work earnestly, to speak kindly, to act sincerely, to choose thoughtfully that course which occasion and conscience demand; to be womanly always; to be discouraged never; in a word, to be loyal under any and all circumstances to my Fraternity and her highest teachings and to have her welfare ever at heart that she may be a symphony of high purpose and helpfulness in which there is no discordant note. Written by Ethel Switzer Howard, XI Chapter, 1904

But it wasn't until months after that that Steve and I began to develop a friendship. I was 21, the legal age to attend the Mardi Gras Ball in Mobile, so we went on our very first friend-date just to have some conversation. I was so nervous; I could not even eat my pasta at Olive Garden. Then we went to see the movie *Toy Story* while our friends anxiously awaited our arrival at a local campus hot spot to hear all of the details about how it went. I felt like I was in the movie *Grease*, getting pulled by the girls. Steve and I were just friends, but all of his friends (who were becoming my friends) thought otherwise. Steve and I looked so much alike, too, that people kept asking if we were brother and sister. Steve laughed all throughout the movie, and I thought: *I don't know about this guy. He is just an interesting fellow—and too happy.*

I know, *right*? I don't even know what to say.

Our friendship continued to develop. Long nights of just talking on the phone helped me learn more about him and his Asian culture. I blew his mind when I shared with him that, where I come from, you go "frogging," and then you fry up the frogs and eat them. At the time, I didn't know he had a love for frogs—in fact, he had a pet frog in college named Rasputin—so needless to say, he was a bit in shock about the whole thing. Especially the eating part.

I found it incredibly easy to talk to Steve. I wanted to be honest with him and tell him that I enjoyed his friendship, but I had recently ended a long relationship, and I just didn't want to go there. The last thing I wanted, I thought, was to step into another relationship. Turns out, he felt the same because he had just left a relationship, too. He still jokes with me today that the real reason I moved to Alabama was to find a husband.

Steve began to write me beautiful poetry as he waited for me to walk to our next classes together. He even published one of them, called "First Kiss," and posted it for the entire campus to see. I kept thinking, *Why are you doing this to me?* The truth was, I didn't think I was worthy of such love from another person. I was still carrying a lot of shame and guilt from my previous relationship about the fact that I had put up a wall around my heart that even a sledgehammer could not penetrate. I started to pull back somewhat, and retreat inside myself as the relationship seemed to pull me in. I'd escape to my favorite place, the beach, with my sorority sisters.

Over time, though, I began to shift. My feelings for Steve were growing, and I couldn't help thinking that maybe he was the right person for me after all. I'll never forget the day I was bringing out the trash, and Steve was standing with a group of guys in his white Gap tee, Gap jeans, and Timberlands. His hair was long, he had no glasses at the time, and he smiled the most beautiful smile. My heart skipped a million beats. That was new! He asked me what I was doing that night and invited me to go to the hockey game with the new group of friends I had met the night I arrived.

Steve and I continued our friendship over the next few months, spending a lot of time together. A year and a half later, Steve proposed to me, and I said, "Yes." We waited for another year and a half before we married.

On January 23, 1999, I married the man of my dreams. But what we didn't know was that the next chapter of our lives was about to be the roughest roller coaster ever. It would either make us or break us—there would be no in-between. As I continued to wrestle with illness, addictions, and severe depression, Steve was swept along for the ride and found himself fighting for his life, his marriage, and the woman he loved. It was difficult for him to watch me self-destruct and feel so hopeless. He was at risk of losing everything that mattered to him. How could he get me back without giving up? I was difficult to handle. Triggers would result in rages or silence with no in-between. My heart walls were pretty thick, and I had no intentions of letting him in.

CHAPTER 4

THE FAMILY

There is a sacredness in tears. They are not the mark of weakness,
but of power. They speak more eloquently than ten thousand tongues.
They are the messengers of overwhelming grief, of deep contrition,
and of unspeakable love.
~ Washington Irving

*I*n 2000, a year after Steve and I were married, we started talking about whether we wanted to have a baby. Steve mentioned that he had read an article that said that if a woman wants to conceive and her thyroid is out of balance, it can lead to miscarriages. I made an appointment with an endocrinologist to see about my thyroid. The doctor ended up diagnosing me with hyperthyroidism, or overactive thyroid, which typically causes unintentional weight loss, a rapid or irregular heartbeat, and speeded up metabolism. The diagnosis finally provided an explanation for the tremendous weight loss that I had been experiencing. The doctor put me on medication to manage it but advised me that I might have difficulty conceiving if my thyroid continued to be hyperactive. Which, of course, it did.

At the same time, Steve and I had been looking forward to having children together. In early July 2001, I took a pregnancy test, and it came back negative. We were bummed and thought that, given my history of health problems, we might have a long row to hoe to get pregnant. My next thyroid panels and bloodwork results came back in the normal range, but I started to feel tired and run down. Still, the pregnancy tests weren't telling us anything. But, still hopeful, Steve went back and forth to Walmart to get more tests, so we could monitor how things were coming along.

Then, a week later, we got an encouraging sign. I took two pregnancy tests at the same time and then one more the following day—just to make sure. They were all positive.

The first person I called to share the news with was my sister, Shanna. When we finally had certainty that I was pregnant, she and I decided to plan a special weekend with our family to announce the news. The family had still been getting together for family gatherings over BBQ, fish fries, and seafood boils from time to time, but we lived 90 minutes away, so we wanted to plan it in advance and make sure everyone would be present. It would be my parents' first grandchild, and we were excited to tell them. By the time of the party that weekend, I was already starting to show, so of course everyone was excited and certain that I was carrying twins. The strange thing was that, according to the ultrasound, there was only one baby there.

Steve got so excited about becoming a dad that he started writing "Hello I'm Here!" letters, then he'd sign them "From Baby Potter" and have them framed. But I was still in disbelief. I just wasn't feeling like myself. At six weeks, I started cramping. I started feeling nauseous day and night—there was hardly any break from it. I started to get depressed, too: my clothes didn't fit, and I was feeling awful. By seven weeks along, I was already struggling with it. My first prenatal appointment revealed that my blood pressure was elevated. Not good.

By August, my hands started trembling uncontrollably, and my heart palpitations became more noticeable. I made a thyroid appointment, but the bloodwork came back normal, so there was no news there. It was a new school year, and I was an elementary school teacher commuting an hour each way. Because I was a teacher, I was standing all day, and that made my legs really swollen and sore. Then I began to have lower abdominal pain, sciatic nerve pain, and frequent nose bleeds. Then I started vomiting. By the time I was 12 weeks pregnant, the cramping and nausea had gotten worse, and I was completely flattened with exhaustion. My OB decided to do an ultrasound, and we found that the baby's heartbeat was 169, a little above the normal range of 120-160. However, everything via ultrasound looked great. I had nothing to worry about, they said. But I did have a bladder infection, so they started me on an antibiotic. The next four weeks were not so bad, and things were looking up: I was feeling better, and the nausea and cramping had subsided.

By my 16-week appointment, my OB thought that my blood pressure was high again, and I was gaining weight quickly. The baby's heart rate was 140. At 20 weeks, we learned we were going to have a little boy! We were over the moon excited. By 21 weeks, my blood pressure dropped again, and I had gained more weight.

At 22 weeks, I called my doctor because I felt something was wrong. The severe cramping had returned, and I had gone through a major bout of diarrhea and exhaustion. From that day forward, I was put on strict bed rest, with plenty of fluids, and more antibiotics for another bladder infection. I was supposed to continue that way until I felt better, but the symptoms persisted. I was finally admitted into the hospital for treatment of dehydration and infection in my colon.

By 24 weeks, my body was retaining too much fluid. My feet and legs were terribly swollen. I was told I could go back to work, but a week later, I started having dizzy spells that made me feel like I was going to faint. I did a 24-hour urine test, which, among other things, measures the protein in the urine and the kidney function. If protein is spilling into the urine, it can cause preeclampsia, a dangerous complication of pregnancy that comes with symptoms of high blood pressure and sometimes some sort of organ damage. My test results at the time were showing in the normal range, so at least that was encouraging.

At 28 weeks, I was put back on bed rest with another 24-hour urine collection and more bloodwork to do. My OB got concerned about my high blood pressure and nausea, which was back in full force. Ultrasound was performed as a precaution, and we learned that our son was fine and did not show any signs of distress.

At 30 weeks, I started having what felt like contractions. The following week, I was diagnosed with preeclampsia. I was also diagnosed with edema, pregnancy-induced hypertension, and anemia. I had reached 190 pounds; I was 45 pounds heavier than when I got pregnant.

At 33 weeks, I was doing 24-hour urine tests every week. We needed to watch the results because anything over 300 is dangerous and would require immediate delivery. We were hoping to avoid that. My numbers were climbing, so we were worried. I had already signed my consent for a C-section if I needed to deliver early, just in case. After all, I was considered high-risk. The nausea, headaches, pressure, and abdominal pain were intense. I began leaking amniotic fluid, so they checked to see if my amniotic sac had ruptured. It hadn't, thank goodness. I also had some bacteria testing done to see if that was causing preterm labor. The nausea was thought to be due to gallbladder issues, but the gallbladder ultrasound came back showing there were no problems. Of course.

At 34 weeks, a nonstress test, which monitors the baby's health and heart rate to see if there are any signs of distress, was done, and the results were fine. My 24-hour urine came back normal, too. Then, on February 14, 2002, I started having contractions. I was admitted into the hospital to stop them, and then I was sent home to be monitored. The protein count had climbed to 290, knocking on that 300 door, and it scared the hell out of Steve and me. Four days later, I weighed 201 pounds, and my OB told me she wanted to induce labor at 37 weeks.

Already on bed rest, I was sent to my parents' home to await the birth because we lived so far away from my doctor and the hospital. We didn't live near the hospital, and we wanted to make sure I could quickly get there if I went into labor. The next day, the weather outside was severe. We had a dramatic display—a downpour with lightning and thunder. I was feeling a strange sensation in my abdomen that I didn't understand, along with extreme pain and nausea, and I figured I had to just endure it. The only thing I could do was put on my headphones and listen to music. I just couldn't get enough of Kid Rock's, "Only God Knows Why."

I was able to make it through the night, but the next morning, something felt terribly wrong. My baby was not moving, and I was scared to death. I started to cry, telling mom and dad I needed to go to the hospital—NOW. I made it to Labor and Delivery at 8:20 a.m., where they hooked me up to the monitors and eventually found the baby's heart rate—which was doing just fine. However, we could not get him to move.

What I did not know at the time was that my baby was slowly dying. I asked the hospital staff to please call my OB, but they told me that she was not on call and not available to be reached. So they sent the on-call doctor to my room.

"There is nothing wrong with you," she said when she walked in the door. "You should go home and make an appointment with your doctor."

Needless to say, that did not sit well with me. I threw a tantrum that a two-year-old would be proud of.

"I'm not leaving the hospital. Call my doctor!"

God must have taken over from there because, five minutes later, my doctor walked through the door, having no idea I was even there. The baby's heart rate had dropped to 65 and was still falling. I freaked out. The doctor was livid that no one called her even though my chart had the note that I was a high-risk patient. She ordered an emergency C-section.

I felt bad for my husband. He had been called and was on his way, trying desperately to make it to the delivery in time to be in the operating room with me. In his stead, my mom suited up to be there with me. When Steve finally got there, the doors had already closed because my doctor didn't want to waste any time. She was in the middle of cutting me open, even before my epidural was in effect. (Yes, I could feel it.) She needed to get the baby out immediately, or we were going to lose him.

On February 20, 2002, Brynin Wellington Potter was born at 2:01 p.m., weighing 4 pounds, 14 ounces. He was 17 inches long. I wasn't given a chance to see him at first because he wasn't breathing yet, and the pediatrician and a team of nurses were working hard, trying to save his life. Finally, they were able to stabilize him enough to get him to the NICU. Somebody rolled him out so I could see him from afar, but all I could see was a tiny foot, white as a sheet of paper. Then, after they stitched me back together, I was rolled out, too, and Steve came over to me. He bent over to me, and we just sobbed uncontrollably. I whispered to him, "He is very sick." We shared a moment together that will never be forgotten or broken.

I found out later that my placenta had indeed abrupted due to my preeclampsia, and that my hyperthyroid condition had possibly increased my chances of having preeclampsia in the first place. They told me that Brynin was bleeding out inside of me. They called it a maternal-fetal transfusion, so I had to be closely monitored, too.

They listed Brynin in critical condition and said he would most likely not survive to the next day. He had jaundice, apnea—meaning, his breathing stopped—and bradycardia, a terrible drop in his blood-oxygen level. Should he survive, they said, he would most definitely end up with special needs due to a lack of oxygen to the brain. He had apparently lost 90% of his blood volume and needed blood and platelet transfusions. That's when members of our own family helped out in amazing ways. My dad donated platelets and Steve and my cousin Chris donated blood for Brynin. He was proving himself to be a miracle baby already.

He was quite the little fighter. He was lifeless at first, but around 2 a.m. that morning, when Steve went to check on him, he had started moving his arms and pulling out his tubes and IVs. After one week, he was able to breathe on his own. When he was nine days old, I was finally able to hold and feed my son for the first time. The jaundice was completely gone, and so were the apnea and bradycardia. They took several brain scans, which all came back normal. He was quite the celebrity at the hospital. Everyone knew we had delivered the miracle baby. Finally, on March 6, 2002, 14 days after he was born, Brynin was released from the hospital.

After the delivery, I started to experience post-partum depression. My anxiety was at an all-time high. My physical condition started to deteriorate: the palpitations were out of control, and emotions of fear, depression, profound sadness, mood swings, and uncontrollable crying set in. The doctors just kept medicating me, and I didn't object because I needed a fix to hide the pain. I was on antidepressants during the pregnancy, but they were no longer working after the pregnancy. When I saw the doctors, they told me nothing was wrong with me. All of my pain and confusion was in my head, they said. It was just more insult added to injury.

And so marked the beginning of my experience as a prescription drug addict. I needed pain medication and antidepressants to help me cope with my mental, physical, and emotional pain. I was great at doctor-shopping, too. I learned how to get doctors to change and increase dosages because, after all, they would help me go numb. Plus, each one would just stop working after a while, so I'd either need more of it, or I'd need something to replace it. I mixed up the meds, and I didn't care. I was selfish, yet I self-sabotaged at the same time.

For quite a while after Brynin was born, I went through a very dark time. I struggled just to stay alive. I had black eyes and pale skin; I was thin and got used to living with heart monitors. I was just waiting for my heart to just stop. I had run up all of the credit cards as I kept up with my prescription fixes and doctor shopping with all of the labels that the doctors used to "diagnose" me. I just wanted to die. I begged God to end it all. *Just take me so it would go away,* I told Him. I honestly didn't care anymore. I was so sick and tired of being sick and tired. *FU, devil! You win!* I can't do this anymore! I was done with putting a show on every day, letting people think I was okay when I wasn't at all. I pleaded my case with God, telling Him why I was an awful person that did not deserve to live.

On the home front, I had become a hot mess to take care of. Honestly, I was spiraling out of control, and Steve's patience with me was running thin. When my son was one year old, I could not even take care of myself, much less take care of him, too.

Since we lived two hours away from my doctor, we decided to move back to Gibson, where my parents could help take care of the baby and me. So, we moved in with my parents for the time being. It was definitely a low point in our lives and in our marriage in just about every way. After all, who wants to move back in with their parents? *No one! Ever!* Meantime, Steve struggled to find and keep a job in the area, and our finances weren't in good shape. It also wore on him to hear the rumor mill about us—after all, we were the talk of the town. Oh boy, the trash talk that went on behind our backs. He heard that people were saying that he was no good and couldn't take care of his wife or raise his child, that he was lazy, and a freeloader. I was too self-absorbed to know that he was hurting and had his own hardships. People were casting stones at us and pretending that they lived in a glass house.

But life went on. I wasn't "looking" sick anymore, and, aside from my health being unstable, things seemed to be looking up for us somewhat. Steve and I both were back at work, trying to decide where to live so we could move out of my parents' place. I was still riding a rollercoaster of depression, but we started to think that having another child was doable years later.

At one of my wellness doctor visits, Steve and I wanted to discuss the potential risks of having another child with my OB/GYN. We wanted another child, but we were wondering what it all meant, considering Brynin's birth and the fact that I was now in my 30s. My doctor pointed out that I would likely be considered high risk and would be watched closely because of the way my first pregnancy went. Most likely, the second pregnancy would be "better." So we trusted her opinion and decided to go for it.

In July 2005, we found out I was pregnant with our second child. Just like I had done when I was pregnant with Brynin, I started writing a journal for the new baby. Both times, I wasn't completely sure if I would still be alive to tell them the story of their lives, and I wanted them to know their momma as best I could, just in case. So, I wrote everything down for them. To this day, I have journaled Brynin and Kylie's life. They have stacks to read, and I will continue to write them until the day I die.

Sure enough, I started cramping at four and a half weeks into the pregnancy, so I started seeing my doctor every two weeks after that. I was told I would be okay as long as there was no bleeding. By the time I was at five weeks, the morning sickness started to last all day and night. At eight and a half weeks, the cramping got worse and more painful, so

I booked an appointment with my doctor. From the exam, we found out that there was a tear—the placenta was beginning to separate from the uterus—and there were broken blood vessels that had clotted. I was put on bed rest so the placenta could reattach itself. I never had any vaginal bleeding. I spent the rest of my first trimester on bed rest until I healed. Finally, after that, I was released to go back to work.

But it didn't last very long.

A few weeks later, I started to experience extreme cramping and was rushed to the doctor. The ultrasound showed that the tear had appeared again, except this time it was worse. The doctor had me admitted to the hospital for 24-hour observation and started me on progesterone shots to prevent miscarriage. But the tear still refused to heal. When I was sent home the next day, I was put on strict bed rest again, with Demerol for pain, and was allowed absolutely no moving, except to go to the bathroom. I was re-admitted to the hospital again and again because of fluid loss and was scheduled for D&Cs (dilation and curettage). The ultrasound showed that the baby was absolutely fine.

Finally, I was put in the care of a specialist, who took tests and diagnosed me as having partial placenta previa—a condition when the baby's placenta covers the mother's cervix. At 19 weeks, they stopped my progesterone shots. Two weeks later, they found an extra lobe on my placenta, which needed to be monitored, and at 23 weeks, I started leaking fluid again. The ultrasound showed that there was less amniotic fluid around the baby's feet than there should have been, and the doctor decided to prescribe me an antibiotic again for an infection. Two weeks later, the amniotic fluid level was back to normal, and the specialist released me back to the care of my OB/GYN.

Nobody could give me a clear explanation as to why any of this was happening.

When I was 28 weeks pregnant with my second child, I started leaking amniotic fluid every four hours, so they started monitoring that. Three weeks later, the contractions started up again, I had severe pain on my right side, and my heart rate dropped. The specialist was called again, and I was admitted to the hospital for another 24-hour observation. One more time. The following week, my blood pressure started to climb, my hands, face, and feet began to swell, and I was itching all over without any rash to explain it. The doctor diagnosed the condition as Polyhydramnios, having too much amniotic fluid. Yes, I know. Before, I was losing it and didn't have enough—now, I had too much! It was crazy! An amniocentesis was discussed, but it was decided that it was too risky for me at that point. I was pushing the scale at about 300 pounds.

Once more, I went back to the hospital for another 24-hour observation and a 24-hour urine test. I came home the next day, as expected, but several days later, I was sent back to the hospital because the heart monitor couldn't find a heartbeat for the baby. The hospital did another ultrasound, monitored me through the night, and then sent me home the following day.

They scheduled me for a C-section on February 20, 2006. It happened to be exactly four years to the day that Brynin was born! Both of my babies were born on February 20th, at 35 weeks plus one day. Then, once little Kylie was born, she spent exactly two weeks in the hospital—just like her older brother did—and came home on the same date, too.

Due to the number of tumors they found on my uterus after delivery, I went through a partial hysterectomy six weeks later. My uterus looked like that of a 90-year-old woman and had to come out, they told me. There was also some controversy around my pregnancy because, later, when we investigated my medical documents after my doctor had left her practice, we noticed that there might have been another sac that was never discussed. Interestingly, Kylie believes she had a twin sister, and, as a family, we believe there was another baby, Kamryn Mei.

My two babies are complete miracles from God and the greatest joys of my life. But they entered this world barely thriving—and I was hardly in a condition to parent them. Both nearly died in the womb and outside of it. They were often sick when they were infants; my youngest was in the doctor's office weekly, trying out different antibiotics to see what would work. I had no idea of the immensity of what could come as a result of my actions and choices or the size of the emotional wounds that they would inherit. I believe that my emotional state passed through the placenta, and my babies were receiving emotions they didn't ask for. It was something I carried a lot of guilt for, blaming myself for their difficulties coming into this world and even developmental challenges for a long time.

I was in bad shape. The two traumatic pregnancies I'd endured ignited a war in my body that would take over a decade to unravel and disarm. In the meantime, I couldn't take care of myself, much less take care of two innocent and precious gifts from God. The only way I knew how to deal with my overwhelming feelings was to avoid what I was feeling, avoid my pain, and avoid my self-hatred and feelings of powerlessness. I sought help in medications but found little solace. Sometimes I would cry and beat myself up, feeling like I had abandoned all three of them—the children plus Steve. Due to the emotional chaos that they inherited from me, I felt that I had neglected the children before I was able to hold them. And as for Steve, he had been left with the burden of taking care of the kids while trying to deal with his completely out-of-control wife at the same time.

And so began a downward spiral I wouldn't recover from for many years. The depression was unruly. When Kylie was about five years old, she would sometimes come into my room and open the blinds to tell me it was time to get out of bed because the sun was smiling. But all I wanted to do was pull the comforter over my head and wait for her to leave. I could barely lift my head off the pillow, much less get out of bed or put one foot in front of the other to begin my day. My kids were aware that something was going on.

One minute, I wanted to die—then I would change my mind. I had some severe pain in my spine that no one could explain yet, and it could be so intense that I just wanted to pull all my hair out and scream because it is so unbearable. Sometimes all I could do was sit on the floor, my hair teased and out of control, mascara running down my face. My emotions battled each other. Hope was a distant island. Other times, I'd curl up in a fetal position in the closet and rock back and forth. *Please help me, God. Something is wrong with me, but I don't know what. I am not crazy. That much I know. I just don't know how to pull myself out of this. Please help.*

I had already been diagnosed with depression before I got pregnant the first time, and I was on medication for it throughout both pregnancies and deliveries. But even when I had bad days, I'd go to work the next day teach my elementary students fully composed. No one ever knew what was going for me on the inside—my depression was deepening—and I wasn't about to tell anyone.

As the storm that was brewing inside of me intensified, though, I'd occasionally faint while I was teaching and have seizure-like episodes right during faculty meetings. The doctors said I had low blood pressure, and I needed to increase the salt in my diet. I felt like I was in a freaking nightmare. *Somebody, please wake me up!*

Making matters even worse was that no one understood why I was so emotionally volatile or why I was complaining or depressed. But that ignorance didn't stop a lot of people from voicing their judgments and opinions about me, my life, and my husband. "You are not sick." "You are so thin!" "You sound like a hypochondriac." "You don't look sick—you look great." "You're just being lazy." "You moved back into your parent's home with your husband and child? You're such a freeloader!" "You gained so much weight!" "You are so fat."

And on and on. Being as intuitive as I am, I can read people's energy even before they open their mouths. The whispers and snickers behind my back were awful. The hardest to swallow was when people spat out their judgments about me to other people. I learned people were saying things like, "She's such an emotional wreck, such a weak individual, and just plain *crazy*!" "She is just doing it for attention. She wants everybody to feel sorry for her." They had no compassion and no imagination that someone could be quite ill even if it wasn't obvious on the outside. I finally just got tired of having to justify my struggles to others. I was not crazy; I just wanted to die. It was all seeming to be too much for me. I would rather be alone and not have to deal with anyone at all.

CHAPTER 5

THE BOTTOM

Whoever has experienced near-death
knows how gracious it is to be alive.
~ Lailah Gifty Akita

2003 was another difficult year for me. No one seemed to be listening to me or understanding what I was experiencing physically and emotionally. Many people seemed to think that all my complaining was just a matter of my seeking attention and living off of mommy and daddy. I was terribly depressed; after all, I had been given many chances to get my life together, and I kept failing at it. More and more, I felt that I just wanted to be gone. Problem solved. I figured that it might even be a good thing: my husband and children wouldn't have to bear my painful burdens any longer. The pain pills, antidepressants, and beta-blockers I was on created a devilish cocktail of numbness for me. Sometimes, I wished if I was lucky enough, I would just pass out from it all and never wake up.

One day, when Brynin was just six months old and asleep in his crib, I was in the laundry room right off the kitchen, putting laundry into the washing machine, and fainted. Then something happened that had never happened to me before—and it scared the living daylights out of me.

It was as if I was hovering over my own limp body, looking down at it lying on the floor. *Was I dead?* I wasn't sure. *Why was I floating?* I didn't know. My gray and white cat, Madison, laid beside my lifeless body. Then, I noiselessly moved through the apartment and found Chloe, my other gray cat, inside Brynin's crib with the baby. Apparently, I had not zipped the crib cover properly to keep her out. She was very alert to my presence and watched me intently. She let me know she was protecting him, almost as if he was *her* child.

In a quiet way, I felt some sort of other presence there in the room, but I couldn't tell who or what it was. In the future, under similar circumstances—and yes, there would be more—I'd know exactly who was there with me.

Then, all of a sudden, I was forced back into my body as if someone had picked me up and thrown me back in. As I came to, in my body, I gasped for air.

In the meantime, Steve had been trying to call and check on me. Since I didn't answer the phone right away, he had called a friend of ours who was able to call me and reach me. I told her that I had fainted again—that's why I missed Steve's call. But I didn't dare speak a word of what had really happened —not even to Steve.

After I got off the phone, and while Brynin was still napping, I retreated to my closet. It was my safe place. Sobbing uncontrollably, I curled myself up in a fetal position, not understanding what was happening to me. Then I sat up, letting myself rock back and forth, and said to myself, over and over, "I am not crazy. I am not crazy."

I felt like I had died that day, but even though I had returned, I still felt hopeless, caught in the middle of a tug-of-war between light and darkness. The experience had been quite unsettling to me, and for a while after that, I remained very afraid to die.

My negative, critical thoughts were gaining volume. My mind would almost take on a life of its own, over-analyzing, spiraling down into negativity. Once the negativity started, it was hard to get it to stop. The self-torture seemed constant, which is why I kept going to doctors to try to get new medication that would help cut back the negative thinking. I didn't know anything about holistic medicine back then; in fact, no one I knew did, either. If you had something wrong with you, you'd expect to go see a doctor who would give you a prescription and help you reduce the pain—whatever your problem happened to be. But in my case, every time I went asking for help, they'd tell me that there was nothing wrong with me. I must be crazy.

Who *wouldn't* start to believe that they were losing their mind?

On top of the escalating depression after Brynin's birth, the doctors gave me a new label to feel bad about: "hypermania," a form of bipolar disorder. In addition, my heart was still acting up, so I'd go to see different doctors, but when they hooked me up to a heart monitor, nothing showed except a few hiccups. Finally, someone told me I had premature ventricular contractions, or "PVC," which are extra heartbeats that disrupt the normal heart rhythm and can cause feelings of fluttering or skipped beats. Great.

Sometimes it felt like I was playing the role of a guinea pig for the doctors. They tried this and that, never fully grasping what was wrong with me, practicing what seemed like dartboard medicine. "Here is a beta-blocker. Let's change your antidepressant. Continue the pain med. Have a nice day." It was a mess. But nothing was really helping.

One day it got especially bad. The school I was working for called Steve, telling him I needed help. They reported that I had been acting strange and that something must be wrong. I was slurring my speech, and I could hardly walk at all—as if I didn't even know how to put one foot in front of the other. At the time, Steve was working as a manager at a computer store about a 90-minute drive away. He was the only one on staff there that day, and he wasn't going to be able to get to me quickly enough to take me to see the doctor. Thankfully, my parents were already planning to come up to help out. Steve had called them and told them he needed help, and he didn't know what else to do with me. He was at his wits' end. So they came to drive me to the doctor's office.

By this time, I already had a spinal tap with this particular doctor, but of course, the results came back negative. There I was, back at square one. As awful as I felt, every doctor kept insisting that there was nothing wrong with me. Nobody seemed to believe that I was feeling so poorly. Everybody kept saying, "You look good! You don't look sick!" I was alone, misunderstood, and miserable. Again.

A little while later, I was having some issues, so Steve called the same doctor's office to make an appointment. The physician's assistant listened to how Steve described what was going on and told him, "Oh, okay. Well, you should bring her in." Then, he called my parents and asked if they would pick me up from school and take me to my appointment because he was 90 minutes away.

Once we arrived, I was ushered into an examination room, and just before the doctor came into the room to see me, he turned to the P.A. from the hallway and yelled at her.

"Why did you even allow her to be here?" he bellowed, and I could hear him through the door. "Her test results came back negative, so there's nothing wrong with her. She is a complete nut case, and it's a waste of my time when I could see patients who are in real need!" Then he entered and pretended to be nice about the fact that there was nothing in my spinal tap that indicated any illness. By this time, my parents were fuming. Words were exchanged and we left.

When the appointment was over, and we walked out of his office into the lobby, my mom and dad were so upset, they were going to let the world know it. With colorful language, my parents told the lobby full of patients about his lack of compassion and hurtful manner.

"How could you even work with this man?" they asked everyone sitting there. Even though I was hurt and upset, crying and feeling hopeless, I just wanted to leave as quickly as possible. I hate confrontation; it had turned into the worst of all worlds.

In 2007, I passed out once again in the back room of my parents' home. I floated out of my body, looked around, and—*Bam!*—was thrust back into my physical body again, gasping for air. I felt like I had just been slapped, hard, like a newborn child. My heart rate was erratic when I came to. Since I had been a nursing assistant, I had a stethoscope and blood pressure cuff, so, since I was feeling so weird, I pulled them out and listened to my own heartbeat and took my own blood pressure.

Steve was in another room, so I called to him to tell him something was wrong. I told him my heart was erratic and I needed to go to the hospital. He rushed me to the emergency room, where they hooked me up to an EKG, which displays the activity of the heart and can inform doctors about impending heart disease. When the nurses looked at the monitor, they seemed to be fascinated with what they were seeing. Apparently, the numbers were indicating that I was having a heart attack—but I clearly wasn't because I was completely present and coherent! They looked at me, looked at the monitor, and then looked back at me—not able to make sense of it. Each one took turns to listen for themselves; then they told me they had never seen or heard anything like it before.

The doctor came in, someone we'd never met before, who had no bedside manner whatsoever. He made it clear that he thought that seeing me was a complete waste of his time and that I shouldn't have been there in the first place. "Nothing's wrong with you," he said flatly. "You need to go make an appointment with a cardiologist." I was obviously awake and functioning, so I was wasting his precious time. I needed to go find one more new doctor.

So, I did. I went to another doctor, who put me through all sorts of testing, including an angiogram, but nothing showed up as a problem. They only found out that I was right-side dominant and, if I did ever have a heart attack, it would most likely occur on my right side rather than my left. They chalked it up to the PVC diagnosis and was given different beta-blockers to try. I continued to have fainting spells, and even fainted in the classroom, traumatizing my poor students.

The next four years were pretty much the same. I went back to teaching and tried to get my life back together. I was still on all my medications, but I tried to cover up everything and pretend everything was normal. I wore a smile as a mask to get through the day; I was so tired of dealing with the disbelief and hurtful thoughts. My heart was functioning better, and I needed fewer doctor's visits. It was up and down.

In 2011, my health started to seriously decline again, and with it, my world began to crumble once more. I was teaching in a very, very old building that had a lot of black mold, asbestos, and other toxic substances we've only recently started to take seriously. I was getting exposed to them every single day. I needed the doctors again, as the fatigue was off the scale. The doctors tried changing my antidepressant, switching me from Zoloft to Lexapro to Cymbalta, and tried increasing my dosage again and again, but nothing was working.

Then I went to a new neurologist who diagnosed me with fibromyalgia and chronic fatigue syndrome (CFS). He would be my last neurologist.

This guy was different than any of the other doctors I'd ever been to. Knowing about my bad behavior with meds, he sat down in his chair, slid over to me, positioned himself in front of me knee-to-knee, and looked me dead in my eyes.

"You are one combination away from never opening your eyes again," he said. "Is that what you truly want?"

I just crumbled and sobbed. I didn't need all those pills, he told me.

He was the first doctor to say I wasn't crazy; he was the first one who cared enough to give me a reality check. Finally. Someone on my side.

I realized that I had become great at covering up all my suffering with the help of those pills. Suffering was pretty much all I had known, and I didn't know of any other options to deal with it. I had seen many doctors who had prescribed all sorts of labels and prescriptions, but they were actually contributing to my destruction. They were enablers, considering the number of pharmaceuticals they prescribed to help numb my physical, emotional, and mental pain. But I used them, too. If a doctor did not give me what I wanted, then I would find another one to increase the dosages or prescribe something stronger to stop the physical pain. Then I would just take everything I was prescribed from every doctor I saw. It was just a matter of time before my heart would just stop. Besides, no pharmaceutical in the world can take the pain out of the soul.

I went cold turkey starting that day.

This doctor diagnosed me with fibromyalgia based on my symptoms. Since there's not really an accurate medical test for fibromyalgia, the doctors will make the diagnosis based on your symptoms. So, he started me on a fibromyalgia drug, but it gave me such severe side effects that I had to quit it and decided not to take anything for it. I went through horrible withdrawals, extreme agitation, sweats, vomiting, diarrhea, and complete misery for the first couple of weeks. I don't know how I didn't perish during that time, but I gradually got better.

Yet, I was still being hard on myself and hiding the reality of my life from the world and those I loved. In my mind, it was a punishment for being so out of control. *I deserve to suffer*, I thought. *I put myself into this mess, and now it's time to get myself out of it. No one can help me if I can't help myself. Blah blah blah.*

I knew that I couldn't work in the same building I'd been working in anymore, and I had to figure out something else to do. As I thought about it, I realized that a lot of my students had learning disabilities, and since I had been that way as a child and had to suffer through a lot of it myself, I thought I might be able to help kids in a meaningful way. My son also had severe auditory processing and dyslexia, so I was well-versed in the problems and the solutions. My teaching is multi-sensory in nature anyway, which is especially helpful for dyslexic kids, so it would be a good fit.

I decided to buy a franchise of Dyslexia Institutes of America, a program that helps train short term and long term memory. I loved it, and quite a few of the kids excelled in my class. But then, after about 18 months into the business, my health—my own cognitive health—started to decline again. I couldn't keep up with my paperwork or even remember how to do it; I couldn't remember how to do the testing. Then, my inability to function caused me to spiral down emotionally.

Once again, my emotions took over, and I dove back down into self-pity. I was done. I had to give it up. Two years after I opened the clinic, I had to close it. It was 2013. I packed everything back up and sold it back to the person who sold it to me in the first place. I was horribly embarrassed and never told anyone the true reason for making the choices I made.

Back in 2011, as we were looking for ways to get along financially, Steve and I had joined a multi-level marketing (MLM) company, which sells nutritional supplements and wellness products. I had discovered them at the fitness center I was going to and thought maybe I'd give them a try. Sure enough, I started taking the supplements and felt amazing in the beginning. Then I thought, if I'm feeling good, maybe others can feel good, too.

It was a completely new business model for me—selling products within a larger organization—but more importantly, it was the first time I was introduced to the ideas of personal growth. Honestly, I didn't even know what "personal growth" meant at the time. I always thought "those kinds" of books and worship music were of the devil. If it wasn't traditional "church" music, I didn't want any part of it. But most of the people we met within the organization were Christ-centered, anyway. They talked about bettering yourself instead of blaming yourself and others for your issues. I found myself asking myself something I'd never thought to ask before: *How can I become a better person?* It was brand new to me, and it felt good. I started reading about forgiveness—forgiving oneself as well as forgiving others. It was a start.

Steve and I had been having some marriage difficulties for a while; he was struggling with being married to somebody who's out of control a fair amount of the time! But this new direction turned out to be the beginning of a new road for us. It was the beginning of the healing of our marriage. Forgiveness was probably the first, biggest step in the right direction.

It was 2014, and I still really had no idea what I have been dealing with for most of my life. The symptoms had gotten worse after my first pregnancy, and then, after the second pregnancy, it felt like I had hit a point of no return. In August 2014, someone asked me, "Have you ever heard of Lyme disease?" I hadn't, and no one that I knew had either. I was told that Lyme has been found to be the cause of many mysterious symptoms, but the testing is very unreliable and inconclusive. I did follow someone's suggestion and decided to sit under Rife lights—a healing technology based on frequencies—for 90 minutes set to several different Lyme frequencies. But it thoroughly drained me. I was so freaking sick, I thought death had arrived once again. My reaction to those frequencies sure seemed to prove that I did have Lyme. Plus, I filled out a Horowitz Lyme MSIDS questionnaire by Dr. Richard Horowitz, which asks you if you've had any of up to 38 symptoms of Lyme disease, I ended up with the highest score possible. Yup, in my mind, I knew I had Lyme disease. So I immediately started a yearlong herbal protocol that I hoped would help.

Then I started to learn more about detoxification. I bought an infrared sauna and an ionic foot detox machine to try to get some of the toxins that were hurting me out of my system. But there was a problem: I didn't sweat like most people do, so the sauna didn't help. I later realized that the way my body eliminates toxins—the pathways—were stuck. So, I was constantly killing stuff off, but I couldn't rid my body of it. It just stayed inside me, doing its damage.

"You look like absolute death."

In September 2014, I had gone to my usual hair appointment with my best friend and stylist, Nathan, who I'd been working with for years. He knew me quite well, and he'd been following my journey, so we were anything but strangers. For him to say that, I knew he felt he needed to.

He continued. "You are sick, and you need help. And I'm going to get you help."

Nathan referred me to a chiropractor who offered sessions in a hyperbaric oxygen tank, which had been able to help a lot of people with a lot of different physical issues. He told me that's what I needed to finally start feeling better. But, at the time, I was anti-doctor.

I didn't want to have anything to do with doctors; based on all the trauma and hurt I'd endured due to doctors, there was no way I was going to step into the office of someone with a "D" in their title. Whenever it was suggested, I'd have temper tantrums and get extremely stubborn.

I looked at Nathan sideways, letting him know it wasn't going to happen.

But he was insistent. "I'll drive you there," he said. "You don't have a choice. I've cleared my schedule for the rest of the day, and you're going to get into my car, and I'll take you there."

It turns out that the chiropractor was very passionate and extremely knowledgeable about concussions and brain injuries. I told him that it was suspected that I might have chronic Lyme disease and was on an herbal protocol, and he was okay with that at that time.

Then he said, bluntly, "You are a walking dead woman! Your tissue oxygen saturation is only 9%! Healthy people have at least 95%! You need to get in this hyperbaric oxygen chamber right now!"

I was so scared and upset that I burst into tears. I called my husband, and the doctor explained everything that he had just told me to Steve so could understand it, too. I did a full hyperbaric oxygen therapy (HBOT) session that day. The ammonia stench that came out of my body afterward—a sign of an unhealthy liver—could have blown up the place. I was so embarrassed, yet so toxic.

I was thinking that this doctor could be the Earth Angel I was looking for to help me live again. I gave myself permission to have a glimmer of hope. But ultimately, it would be a false hope.

Throughout the whole ordeal, I also had extreme neck, spine, and back pain. So, I had an MRI scheduled to see what was going on and followed up with traction, heat, and stimulation to help provide some pain relief. My results showed C6-7 disc protrusion with mild cord impingement which worsens slightly with extension positioning, and L Spine with multi disc bulging and congenital fusion of left facets at L3-4. He put me on some nano-nutrients for nutrition and told me he wanted my body to be more alkaline.

Then we ordered an expensive ALCAT test to find out what food intolerances I had. The morning of my test, I called the doctor at 7:30 a.m. and asked him if I could check the "MTFHR" checkbox on the ALCAT form that would make sure I got tested for an active gene mutation that I had been told that most Lyme patients have. He agreed, so I checked the box.

At my next appointment, with test results in hand, he told me he had news for me.

"You have MTFHR Heterozygous 1298C. That's been your problem all along."

What a relief! I thought. *Finally! Some answers!*

He put me on some new supplements for the new problem and started singing a different tune about the Lyme problem. He turned anti-Lyme and many times forced me to listen to long lectures about it even though I didn't agree with him at all. He also told me I didn't need the herbs I was taking, but I didn't stop taking them. My intuition was very strong about that. I wanted to give him credit for being more helpful than any other doctor had been throughout my journey—especially for helping me see that I wasn't crazy and for sharing his knowledge about concussions. Sometimes I thought he genuinely cared, but sometimes a switch would go off, and he would seem to be disconnected from what I needed. All I knew was that there were more pieces to the puzzle, and I was only—maybe finally—getting started. After all, he did introduce me to what it was like to see different perspectives.

And on it went. I had another rough week with terrible insomnia, achy, abdominal swelling, and pain, and then a seizure-like episode that lasted eight minutes. I was miserable. The seizure-like episodes were happening more frequently.

He tested me for concussions and decided that it was best that I not get behind a wheel to drive. Apparently, I had post-concussion syndrome, most likely from having fallen into the engine hole of my dad's boat or the go-cart accident I had when I hit a tree head-on at a high rate of speed. Plus, don't forget the head-banging I'd done for so many years. It all resulted in untreated brain injury, causing more damage.

I continued the HBOT sessions. For over a year, my momma drove me to see him three times a week because I could not drive. Some days were very difficult for her to watch her daughter flailing like a fish on a table and looking lifeless after it stopped. I remember her sobbing. It was probably the first time she really got a glimpse of my life and what I had been going through. Most of it was hidden from my dad and her, and, well, we just didn't talk about such things. Better to sweep it under the rug then express your feelings. I was just an expert at hiding my feelings and emotions.

Eventually, I began to feel somewhat better. I started cryotherapy sessions, too, and even began to work part-time at the doctor's clinic in hopes of continuing treatments more cheaply. But the stress was much more intense than I had realized; driving more than 90 minutes each way, every day, turned out to be just too much for me to handle. I was extremely overwhelmed most of the time.

Not surprisingly, I just couldn't keep up the fast pace or remember everything I was supposed to do, and it was frustrating. I was getting fewer HBOT treatments due to the number of paying patients running through the place—and I wasn't one of them. Once again, I was feeling myself spiraling out of control, back into the darkness.

Then, I started having trouble with my vision. One night, as I was driving the hour and a half drive home, I called Steve, sobbing and terrified. It was dark and raining, and everything was completely a blur. Since I had been getting more confused and sometimes even lost, we had decided to put a tracker app on my phone so he could find me if he needed to. That night, with an abundance of patience, love, grace, and ease, he guided me home. After I got home, I took a shower and then sat down to write in my journal:

> "Thank you, Lord, for Steve! He is an amazing husband, friend, and, most of all, my soul mate. That man loves me unconditionally. I don't know how I deserve this. I am grateful and blessed that You see otherwise. Please protect him and give him peace. I know it's hard for him to be away from his family to provide for us. Amen."

I went to the eye doctor, and my eyes had indeed changed. I needed to wear glasses full time.

I consider 2015 to be the ultimate rock bottom for me. After all of the hyperbaric treatments, along with taking a boatload of nano-nutrients, I was only getting worse. My body was hurting, my symptoms were out of control, and I felt like my life was surely fading away—and I did not want to go back down that road. I had a heavy feeling in my gut and knew I did not have much time left if I continued doing what I was doing. I was only growing weaker each day, all the while trying to keep it all together. I could feel myself dying.

I had gotten quite sick with liver issues and severe pernicious anemia. I had extreme bone pain, migraines, continuous cramping in hands and feet, and severe abdominal pain. Blood tests showed that I had severe vitamin deficiencies, my liver, kidneys, and thyroid, were under-functioning, and I had an iron overload. Even with the HBOT treatments, my blood oxygen levels were only up to 12% since I first started with him a year earlier. I was distraught. I had been doing so much to get better, but I was only getting worse.

In the meantime, in spite of it all, my husband continued to be there for me. One day, he sent me a text that read: "I was looking at the sunrise on the way to work and thinking about what made it beautiful. Well, it was not the sunrise itself, but the whole experience. This is how I feel about my beautiful wife. There is not one thing I focus on you. I LOVE ALL OF YOU!"

Still, I was deeply depressed and trying to manage my debilitating fatigue and exhaustion at the same time. Some days I could barely get out of bed. I was having severe headaches, and the pain was virtually unbearable. Sometimes I had numbness in my face and throughout the entire right side of my body so I could barely walk. I struggled just to put one foot in front of the other and needed assistance to go to the bathroom. There were times when the room I was in would seem to spin around me, and as soon as I started to stand, the nausea would start. Then I'd have shortness of breath and would gasp for air as the pain radiated through the left side of my body.

A friend of mine called me, and I happened to tell her a little bit about what I was going through. She asked to visit, but I was wary. It seemed that every time I honestly shared something about my mental or physical health with somebody, it would turn into an intervention. As for her, my intuition was telling me she was up to something.

But I agreed that she could come for a visit anyway.

Later that day, I was in the kitchen, cooking bone broth on the stove, and I heard her pull into the driveway. When I looked out, I saw that another person had come with her. I don't like surprises, and usually for good reason.

They came inside, we sat at the table, and introductions were made. I was smiling on the outside, but I was fuming on the inside. The "friend" apparently had a whole team on the phone, all primed with the intention to rebaptize me in the name of Jesus Christ. She got up and went around my house, sprinkling holy water and anointing each door with holy oil everywhere, while the others on the phone were speaking in tongues and saying prayers, trying to cast demons out of my home and my soul.

It was like a cyclone had entered my home, with a mind of its own, oblivious to my own desires or needs. Needless to say, it turned out to be more of a deliverance for her too. It was a long night, indeed.

Then I had an experience that was darker than any other I'd gone through. One night, terribly sleep-deprived and somewhat nauseous, I noticed a faint glow in the room I was in. I tried to stand, my arms reaching out to try to touch it, but I collapsed to the floor. In a fetal position, I started rocking and then excessively crying. It felt like I was being hunted. Voices in my head were yelling at me, criticizing me. Negative beliefs and emotions and thoughts consumed my mind. All I could do was repeat the words: "Go away. Leave me alone."

Then the visions began. Millions of spider-like creatures were coming out of the ground and knocking on my doors and windows. Death was approaching. I smelled rotting flesh; the stench was in my house, under my carport, in my car, in the shower, and it would never go away. The sound of "tick-tick-tick" on my window kept repeating, like someone was using their fingernails to knock, insisting that they be let in.

It wasn't a dream; it was completely real. It felt like the enemy was hunting me and ready to devour its kill, but I wasn't budging. I refused to let them in and control me. I had come out of the fires of hell before, I reasoned, and I wasn't giving up again.

All I could do was get down on my knees, pray, and beg God to help me. Over and over, I said, "I love you, Jesus! I love you, Jesus!"

I pleaded with God that night. *I'm so sorry for all of my poor decisions and sins. I don't want to die. Please make it stop, and whatever is hunting me, make it go away.* I made a promise that I would do the necessary work to heal and be a better person. I promised I would open up and let the light in, surrender, and walk in obedience.

I couldn't get any lower than that moment. I was so desperate to be restored that I couldn't see that what I was looking for was within me the whole time. It wasn't anyone else's responsibility to heal me. God had been there all along, but He wasn't going to hand it to me on a silver platter. I had to be still, listen to His instructions, and do the work.

With that understanding, like lightning, all the spiders were wiped out, and the stench was gone.

There was complete stillness and silence.

After a while, I put myself to bed, and when I started to fall asleep finally, I seemed to float up above my body once again. I figured that I just had a crazy, unexplainable event, and this meant I had truly died. I looked down at my body, lying on the bed with my hands on my heart, and I looked like a corpse in a coffin. Floating above it, I felt the presence of two beings enter the room behind me. It was my grandfather on my dad's side and my uncle who had passed when I was a young child—the one whose funeral I missed.

My grandfather reached out his hand to me as my uncle looked on, smiling.

"Mitch," my grandfather said, "let's go for a long walk." He always liked calling me "Mitch" instead of "Michelle."

We were instantly relocated to the house where my grandparents had lived, and I was sitting in the exact spot at the bar that I always sat when I visited them as a child.

"Mitch, you have much work to do," he said. "It's not your time. God has big plans for you. You already know this. You must believe in greatness. You must go back now and follow God's calling for your life. You will know what to do through obedience, and you will be heavily protected. Now, you must go."

We said our goodbyes. My uncle never spoke, only smiled and nodded. But I was able to say goodbye to him that night, which I had not been able to do when I was a girl, and the sadness I had been carrying from his death was finally released.

Completely exhausted, I fell asleep finally, without fear of being terrorized, and with a sense of peace. Thankfully, my husband was away at work, and my children were asleep, so no one else had been affected by the hellish events of the evening.

When I woke up the next morning, I was drawn to remember my grandpa's passing. My dad and I had stood next to his bedside the day he took his last breath. It was Christmas Day, and the snow was coming down outside of his window. Other family members were in the kitchen. Grandpa's eyes were open, and he wanted a sip of water. He looked at Dad, then at me, and I felt his connection. I held his hand and told him how much I loved him. Then, he closed his eyes. I returned to the kitchen to let the rest of the family know that Grandpa was slipping away. They gathered around him and, just a few minutes later, Grandpa left this world to begin his journey home to our Heavenly Father.

So, on September 8, 2015, I made the decision to take control of my own health and begin a new healing journey. After many failed attempts with the medical community, I decided there had to be a better way to health. Pills just chase symptoms; I saw that first-hand. I wanted something that would get to the root and allow the branches to crumble. I thought this new path might be the one I need to truly heal. I enrolled at Trinity School of Natural Health to become a board-certified Traditional Naturopath via their book program. In 2018, I received my full certification.

CHAPTER 6

THE SHIFT

You either get bitter or you get better. It's that simple. You either take
what has been dealt to you and allow it to make you a better person,
or you allow it to tear you down. The choice does not belong to fate,
it belongs to you.

~ Josh Shipp

*L*et's review. Over the years, I had been diagnosed with Chronic Fatigue Syndrome; Neurally Mediated Hypotension (NMH); depression; hyper-mania; Irritable Bowel Syndrome (IBS); hyperthyroid and hypothyroid individually, and then later, became Hashimoto's, anemia, Epstein Barr virus; fibromyalgia; MTHFR Heterozygous 1298C, plus quite a few other genetic mutations; concussion; mold syndrome; continuous cold; upper-respiratory conditions; flu diagnoses. About $600,000-worth of misdiagnoses later, someone finally suggested I research chronic Lyme disease. I had no idea that it even existed.

Lyme disease is the fastest-growing infectious disease in the U.S., according to the International Lyme and Associated Disease Society. There are an estimated 329,000 new cases of the hidden epidemic each year in the United States, according to the CDC, but I personally believe the numbers are much higher. I was actually told by a doctor that Lyme disease did not exist in the state of Louisiana. He didn't know what he was talking about. The magnitude of the disease still bears too many unanswered questions about its impact on human health. The types of treatments that are recommended by the medical establishment usually consist of antibiotics as well as suggestions by uneducated people who cannot even pronounce the name correctly half of the time.

First, let's get the name right. It's *Lyme* disease—*not* "Lyme's" disease. This nightmare's ulterior motive is to kill its host with a painful and slow death. It eventually breaks a person down to their core and rots out their insides and eventually breaks down their organs. It takes away their quality of life, creates emotional distress, spreads and hides in different parts of the body; it is highly intelligent, and its ultimate objective is to kill its host in the most painful, slowest, and most deceitful way possible so that their death certificate reads: "Died of natural causes."

According to the Center for Disease Control, Lyme disease is the most common "vector-borne" disease—that means transmitted to humans by mosquitos, ticks, and the like—in the United States. They say it's caused by a bacteria and transmitted from blacklegged ticks. Typical symptoms, according to the CDC, are fever, headache, fatigue, and a characteristic skin rash that looks like a bullseye. If left untreated, the infection can spread to the joints, the heart, and the nervous system. The CDC also claims that most cases of Lyme disease can be successfully treated with a few weeks of antibiotics, but I'm guessing they don't know anybody with Lyme. Other sources list the following as common symptoms of Lyme disease:

- Bladder dysfunction
- Buzzing, ringing, or pain in the ears
- Chest pain or rib soreness
- Confusion
- Constipation or diarrhea
- Depression
- Difficulty concentrating or reading
- Difficulty walking
- Difficulty with speech or writing
- Disorientation
- Disturbed sleep: too much, too little
- Double or blurry vision
- Exaggerated symptoms or worse hangover from alcohol
- Facial paralysis
- Fatigue, tiredness
- Forgetfulness
- Headaches

- Heart palpitations, pulse skips, heart block
- History of heart murmur or valve prolapse
- Increased motion sickness, vertigo
- Joint pain or swelling
- Light-headedness
- Mood swings, irritability
- Muscle pain or cramps

- Neck cracks or neck stiffness
- Poor balance
- Sexual dysfunction
- Shortness of breath or cough
- Sore throat
- Stiffness of the neck or back
- Swollen glands
- Testicular or pelvic pain
- Tingling, numbness, burning, or stabbing sensations

- Tremors
- Twitching of the face or other muscles
- Unexplained breast milk production; breast pain
- Unexplained fevers, sweats, chills, or flushing
- Unexplained hair loss
- Unexplained loss or gain of weight
- Unexplained menstrual irregularity
- Upset stomach

Then, with Lyme, on top of all the physical distress, you begin to break down mentally. Research shows that tick-borne illnesses frequently cause serious mental health symptoms, and in fact, it's often a mental health practitioner that is the first to detect an underlying organic illness. So the illness can make you crazy literally and figuratively! Meantime, doctors and the rest of society think you are a nut case.

I was freaking losing my mind.

Making matters lightyears' worse is the fact that diagnosing Lyme is a very slippery act. The available testing methods measure for an antibody response—not for the infection itself. As a result, testing can often come back with false positives or false negatives. In other words, even after getting tested, you don't know if your test result is telling you the truth. And there are other complications. If someone has a suppressed immune system—which is probably common in those with Lyme—or if they have an infection that wasn't included in the test search, they could get a false negative reading and be told they don't have it. One report says that as much as 56% of patients with Lyme disease test negative using the two-tiered testing system recommended by the CDC. Another report says that 52% of patients with chronic disease get a negative result with the ELISA test, which tests for antibodies, but they get a positive result from the Western "blot" test, which tests for proteins. I could not get a positive CDC Lyme test because my condition was classified as a chronic case and did not meet the CDC requirements. In other words, the tests are basically useless! And, the CDC's reporting that over 300,000 people get Lyme every year doesn't account for all those who are unable to get an accurate read from their test. The number is surely much more.

So, after years and years of trying to get help, only to have medical doctors run me around—*Oh, there's nothing wrong with you; you're psychotic; you need to be admitted to a psych ward, and, by the way, here are some drugs to take; and, oh, by the way, here is a list of side effects for each medication. Okay, see you back in a month*—I felt like I had been through a hurricane and was just spit out. I was depleted in every possible way. I needed better answers.

In August 2014, when Maw Maw told me that she remembered that I got a tick bite as a child and I discovered that Lyme disease comes from tick bites, I started to grab for a small sense of hope again. I had a possible label for everything that was going wrong in my body and that actually made sense to me, so I started to dig into research about Lyme disease and its coinfections. I started to feel a huge sense of relief. The weight seemed like it might be lifting after all. I thought, *Who is crazy now?? It's so not me!!*

I thought, *Now that I know what's wrong with me, I can just do what needs to be done, and all will be well! I like details, and I want to know all there is to know about something!* So I bought the book, *Why Can't I Get*

Better? by Richard Horowitz. I answered his questionnaire and could relate to just about every question. I remember calling Steve to tell him: Finally! This is it! I know this is what is wrong with me! But that night, we disagreed. He wasn't on board. We had been through so much, and my hopes were up. I wasn't going to give up.

I have to admit, though, that he was partially correct. This beast is just not that simple. It spawns coinfections, which are damaging in themselves, plus parasites, autoimmune issues, and it can even ignite gene mutations. Every person who has it most likely suffers in their own unique way. But then, I felt I could perhaps begin to put the pieces of my life together. It was beginning to make sense to me, and I could start believing that I was not such a mental case, after all.

In November 2015, I took a highly sensitive T-cell-based test taken for Lyme that came back positive for Borrelia burgdorferi, which, until 2016, was the only known cause of Lyme disease. (Incidentally, we've since tested Brynin and Kylie, and they both tested positive for "congenital" Lyme disease, which is transmitted from the pregnant mother.)

We stopped working our MLM business and began to try to deal with the fact that I had Lyme. We didn't know what it meant or how we should feel. Should I be happy? Should we celebrate? Could I get some good treatment? Sure, I finally had a beautiful label, all cute and decorated with a bow, and the gift of finally given some clarity and being told that this is what has been causing my misery most of my life.

I finally stopped working with the chiropractor in December 2015 because I realized the treatments weren't helping me get any better. When Steve and I showed him the paperwork that said that I did indeed have Lyme, he just shot us down again and dismissed everything we had to say. So we walked out and never looked back. I have no regrets. I knew it was just one of the many stops on the path least walked. I was grateful for what did work and for the experiences that helped to provide more pieces to the puzzle. But I knew I had to continue on my path to find more puzzle pieces.

Back in 2014, I had started to figure out that seeing a medical doctor wasn't going to get me anywhere. My condition was chronic, which meant that it wouldn't show up on the traditional tests for Lyme, and the docs would never admit that I had it. So, I decided to start following the Cowden Protocol, a do-it-yourself set of herbal extracts that are believed to act as broad-spectrum remedies against Lyme, exerting antibacterial, antiviral, antiparasitic, and antifungal effects.

I kept up with the Cowden Protocol for nine months and later restarted it for round 2, but, as the months went by, it seemed it just wasn't working for me. In the meantime, I tried to find a hematologist to work with because my blood was so bad. It was dark and thick, but noone would work with me. They told me that unless I was diagnosed with cancer and had health insurance, there was nothing they could do for me. I was desperate once more.

By January 2016, I finally found a Lyme-literate medical doctor (LLMD), a doc who is familiar with the long list of symptoms of the disease and aware of its potential coinfections and other complexities that invariably come with it.

Steve and I agreed that I'd work with him for six months to see if I got anywhere. I had a hard time saying yes to it, though. My intuition was telling me not to do it, that it was going to take me out, but I was just too desperate, and I couldn't see that I had any other choices. So, I was willing to give it a shot.

At the time of my first appointment with him, my symptoms were pretty intense. The doctor's approach was to treat two types of bacterial infections—two common coinfections—of Lyme that he felt I was showing symptoms for: Bartonella and Babesia. The treatment was to pulse four antibiotics at a time into my system every four to six weeks. But every time I went in for a doctor's visit, he would give me a new set of prescriptions to treat the infections. He put me on Ciprofloxacin, Flagyl, Malarone, Rocephin, Amoxil, Doxycycline, Minocycline, and Azithromycin. There may have been more. He also gave me Diflucan, an antifungal, because I had systemic candida from the antibiotics. I also had awful rashes all over my body.

At that point, I was feeling so horrible, I could hardly tell which were the symptoms of Lyme, which were symptoms of the coinfections, and which were side effects from all the medications I was on. On the outside, I looked like death warmed over. Again. My skin was pasty, and the dark circles under my eyes were all sunken in. I was extremely fragile in mind, body, and spirit and soul. I had an appointment to discuss with the doctor the idea of inserting a PICC line, a soft tube that is inserted into a vein to provide an entry point for a long series of IV antibiotics. I even met with some of the other patients who had PICC lines and were willing to help encourage me to get the procedure done. But I could just not say yes to it. I canceled my appointment and never went back. I just kept thinking there must be something out there to help me get through the muck. My gut was destroyed, and I was sick and tired of dealing with systemic candida and the side effects of the pharmaceuticals. I cried and prayed that there must be a different way to go about it.

The treatments were wreaking havoc, making me weaker. The pulsing antibiotics treatments made me really ill; I could barely get off of the couch; just lifting my head became a task. The problem is that antibiotics kill every type of bacteria in the body—the good along with the bad. Excessive antibiotics can lead to the growth of resistant bacteria, in other words, the body gets too smart for the treatment, the antibiotics can't kill off the bacteria, and the original problem only becomes more elusive to treat. I felt my doctor was over-prescribing them. Antibiotics don't kill viruses. And, although I didn't know it at the time, I had a high viral load that was wreaking havoc on my system. Meanwhile, my immune system was shut down and unable to defend anything. Everything was at war with everything else inside my body. It was torture.

But that wasn't all. I was also having "Herx" reactions, named for a shortened version of one of the dermatologists that discovered it. It's when the antibiotics kill the bacteria faster than the body can eliminate it; the dead bacteria just keeps circulating, creating a buildup of toxic waste. Which, of course, makes all the symptoms a lot worse—long before they get better.

Knocking on death's door seems to be my specialty all of these years, and quite frankly I needed to change my attitude and perspective on healing.

Then, in July 2016, while I was scrolling through a Lyme Facebook group, I saw conversations discussing a clinic in Mexico that treated Lyme disease specifically. I was desperate to get out of the States, where getting real help and finding doctors who believe you are quite the joke. I was tired of the American medical model of chasing doctors and playing a Roulette wheel of prescriptions; I was tired of listening to anyone else who happened to have an opinion about some type of cure for Lyme.

I was ready for a change. It seemed right. It felt right. I was going to do it.

But Steve and I were financially strained at the time. He had a high-paying job that required him to be on the road nine months out of the year, but we really couldn't see how we could afford it. Given the cost of the program in Mexico, we were going to need a miracle to be able to pay for it. I prayed to God, acknowledging that, if this was a path, He wanted me to take, then He would open the door for us and make it possible. We knew it would take God to make this miracle happen.

On a wing and a prayer, we went to the bank to talk to somebody about how they might help us and found that we could mortgage the house to get some money to help pay for the trip. We were thrilled that we could do that ourselves; we didn't need to have anyone else putting their name on the documents to help us out. But while the bank agreed to give us a loan, it wasn't going to be enough for the full amount of the program and the treatments, much less any extras that we couldn't even predict in advance. There was a high likelihood that I would need to be admitted to the hospital while I was there since nobody knew if my veins would hold up through the treatment. Plus, once we got the results back from their extensive lab testing, I knew that my treatment program might need to change—and all that would take more money, too. The loan would only cover the cost of the treatment plan they set up for me before I arrived. We would have to figure out the rest on our own.

Steve started a GoFundMe campaign online, and, to our amazement, and with our hearts full of gratitude, we were able to raise the rest of the funds we needed to put me through the program and pay for my treatments and hospital visit. The rest of what we would need—money for food, electricity, and renting a place to live for five weeks—that would be up to us. The clinic—which was called Lyme Disease Mexico at the time but has since changed its name to Lymexico—believed that their patients need to stay in a place that is healing for them. Steve and I made arrangements to stay at an oceanfront condo they recommended.

Before leaving for Mexico, I spoke with my doctor by phone to go over my whole history to that point—my autoimmune issues, treatments, protocols, and more—more than 20 years' worth of details.

He was concerned about the anemia and said that I might need to do a bone marrow biopsy, but we would determine that based on my labs taken there. Besides, the LLMD I'd been working with in the States had just finished treating the Babesia with a variety of anti-malaria drugs. The new labs didn't show that I had it, so we opted not to do it. I also had an MRI to make sure I did not have any brain lesions, and it came back pretty clear.

In the meantime, I also filled out a comprehensive questionnaire about diagnoses and symptoms for them. Here is an incomplete list of the items I checked off:

- Abdominal pain
- Anxiety attacks
- Burning sensations
- Confusion
- Decreased concentration
- Depression
- Diarrhea
- Dizziness
- Fainting
- Fatigue
- Headaches
- Involuntary jerking
- Irritability
- Irritable bladder
- Mood swings
- Motion sickness
- Nausea
- Nightmares
- Numbness
- Poor balance
- Sleep disturbances
- Tearfulness
- Tingling
- Unusual clumsiness
- Urinary frequency

Finally, the necessary labs had been completed; our passports were ready to go; our bags were packed. On October 2, 2016, we left to begin our five-week journey to healing in Puerto Vallarta, Mexico. My attitude was, "Let the new adventure begin." For the first time in my life, I felt a sense of peace as I embarked on a very new kind of journey.

When we arrived, sure enough, the views of the ocean from our condo were spectacular, with beautiful sunsets and cruise ships coming and going out of port. I watched the people enjoying their parties and loud music on the decks of the ships as they would pass and thought, "Wow. It must be great to be so carefree and living life to the fullest!" I, on the other hand, was struggling to survive and to make the best possible memories with my family because I didn't know if I would be here much longer.

Could the Lymexico program actually help me get to a point where I could help myself? Or would my body just give up because it was too tired to continue living?

Right away, I began meeting with the staff to get some information about what I should expect in my program. I also got to meet other patients who were there for either Lyme or cancer, many of whom had been suffering as much as I had. I made several friends I'd keep for life. One of my friend's mom took care of me as if I were her own child when the nurses couldn't get my veins to cooperate. Everyone's treatment protocol was unique to them, which, to me, meant that they were addressing issues more precisely than otherwise, and that gave me another sense of hope, too.

My actual treatments began after the testing was completed, nine days after my arrival. Comprehensive bloodwork was done on my appointment day with the doctor, and the labs were sent off to Mexico City specifically to reconfirm that I had chronic Lyme disease. Through weekly live blood analysis—drawn from the capillaries of my ears—and blood labs, I was diagnosed with Bartonella bacteria, parasites, Epstein Barr virus, and certain microbials. I did not receive my results of the Lyme testing until the end of treatment, right before we left to come home. No surprise there: they came back positive.

While the location was beautiful, the treatment experience was pretty brutal. I was bruising, nauseous, and vomiting, and I felt so weak that some days I could barely walk to the elevator. My veins had been collapsing as I had expected, and I couldn't take the endless "sticks" anymore, so I had a chest port put in that they could use to insert the treatments. The taxi rides back and forth to treatment were a nightmare because the brick roads were terribly bumpy, and my chest port did not like all of the bouncing. Plus, everyone was driving crazy. I had to try not to sweat because the last thing I needed to develop was sepsis on top of everything else.

One of the worst things about it was that my family had to witness the terrible shape I was in and all that I suffered through. My husband, my children, my best friend at the time, her fiancé, her daughter, and my mother-in-law had to watch all that I had to endure while not being able to control anything about it. It was very hard on them, and I worried for them.

Some days, when we had time, Steve and I would hang out on the balcony, and I would lay my head on his chest to hear the sound of his heartbeat and so he could hold me and tell me that everything was going to be okay and that we will get through this once again.

Steve was nothing short of an angel. In addition to having to keep up with his work every day, sometimes 24-hour outages for work with no sleep, he never left my side. He held my hand when I needed him, wiped my tears away, gave me words of encouragement, bathed me regularly, even wrapped my port so water wouldn't touch it. He held my hair when there were signs I might vomit and washed it for me because there were some days I barely had the strength to stand in the shower. Being a person who could read souls through people's eyes, I saw his soul. I saw that he hurts because I hurt and that his love for me is immeasurable. The look of love he gave me there was the same look he gave me standing on the stairwell of our dorm complex in college. Steve, I will always forever love you, stars and moon.

I was sent home with eight weeks' worth of Dendretic Cell Vaccines, T-cell activators, an antiparasitic protocol, and another antibiotic combination protocol.

I was better. The night before we left to go back home, I was able to walk and have a sit-down dinner with my family to celebrate. There was no shortage of laughter and smiles that night. I had survived, and I was ready to face the next chapter of my life with persistence. Make no mistake, I was completely exhausted from sometimes 10-, 12- and 24-hour days, of continuous treatment. We made a decision as a family that I would do the necessary work to get better regardless of what happens to me.

I figured time would tell if I would get better once I got home. It did take more than three months to start to regain some type of normalcy for me. I was still experiencing some symptoms, and my doctor and I had follow-up calls. He suggested I needed to focus on my lymphatics to remove the waste and toxins from my body. He also suggested certain herbs to help the process along. With that additional focus, I began to feel much better.

I even started to feel extremely hopeful about my future. I took the huge amount of information I had learned and started researching methods to propel my journey forward. It was a road to recovery that I took on with persistence and dedication.

One highlight of my treatment program in Mexico was my work with a therapist. It was the first time I had ever been exposed to facing and addressing some of the trauma I've experienced in life. It was the first time I let my walls down and began to share things in my life that had been bottled up inside me for so long. For most of my life, I had dismissed a lot of people who didn't seem genuine to me and who I didn't feel I could trust. Being able to read people's energy, I held back from expressing my heart because I could sense the judgment within them and retreat into my corner of shame. But in Mexico, I saw that the therapist knew nothing about me and had no reason to judge, so, for the first time, I was able to trust someone enough to open up and share.

It felt great. I could feel the release of burdens that I carried, even though I knew it was only the tip of an iceberg. It was the beginning of a very new journey for me as I began to awaken a desire and passion within me to know more about myself—my emotional self and the traumas that have affected me—and how I can heal them at their root. Then, I can help others through this process, too.

If the opportunity ever arises, I would go back to Lymexico for a maintenance program in a heartbeat. The program did wonders for bringing me clarity, hope, some healing, and a new direction.

CHAPTER 7

THE REBIRTH

Like a lotus plunging to the surface of a pond
to embrace the light
from its muddy darkness,
truth always rises with time.
~ Suzy Kassem

Two years before I went to Mexico, I had a vision of myself walking in a forest in Washington on some sort of retreat. Columns of light streamed through the trees all around me as I seemed to be traveling a path with a staff in my hand, searching for something. I have never been to such a place in "real life," and I had no idea what it meant at the time, so I tucked it away in my journal.

Then, in 2018, I learned about a company called NES Health, and I was so impressed with their methods and results that I signed up for their Practitioner Training in Tampa, Florida. Before training, I watched live trainings of their Practitioner group, taught by Keith Coley, a NES practitioner at the time and a Chinese medical intuitive who gave lectures on traditional Chinese Medicine and energy healing. I was fascinated with just about everything he talked about. He also mentioned that he and his fiancée, Angel, host a yearly women's retreat within the beautiful forests and beaches of Washington state. As soon as he started talking about it, I got chill bumps all over my body. Something in me was saying, "Ding ding! Remember the vision you had two years ago?"

I had to think about it. Besides offering some wonderful-sounding healing methods, there was another thing that was drawing me: Angel apparently channeled angelic realms, and I was no stranger to unseen forces. I admired her for not being afraid to speak about her experiences and for not letting other people's judgments affect her. I had my own set of "weird talents," having experienced demons, death, rotting flesh, and more. So while I watched others being quick to judge her for her gifts, I wasn't the least bit concerned. Knowing that she had such skills was even a bit of relief for me because I knew she would understand where I was coming from. I was determined to find my true self, and I knew my life would forever change by digging deep into my soul even more.

But even after tossing the pros and cons back and forth, I was still unsure if it was truly the next step for me. I spent the next eight hours in prayer to delve deep into my soul. That's when I began to feel, deep down, that, yes, the idea was indeed God-sent, and I was supposed to attend. I signed up for the retreat without any hesitation after that.

Several months before the retreat was scheduled, I bought some books so I could learn more about Pangu Shengong (PGSG), a form of Qigong, a method they would be teaching at the retreat, and the man who invented it, Master Ou Wen Wei. But reading the books was not easy for me. The energy that they radiated had me vomiting and gave me diarrhea and would make me fall asleep even if I was in the middle of a paragraph! So, I began reading them in tiny sections at a time. I do that even today as I reread them each day! They are energetically powerful.

Finally, in June 2019, I attended Angel-Geschichte's Women's Retreat in Forks, Washington. I loved it beyond measure. Turns out, the area had inspired the location of the Twilight movie series, and it had a very peculiar small-town charm to it. It was quaint. The downside? No internet. I was basically off-grid. The upside? The whole experience made me extremely happy and joyful. Unplugging from the world for a few days of profound healing, learning, and connecting to nature began to heal my soul to a degree I didn't think possible. Between forest bathing, connecting to the beach energy, meditating, group hikes, receiving lessons from Angel-Geschichte, and listening to Keith's lectures on PGSG and women's health—I felt rejuvenated, grounded, and deeply healed on just about every level.

The program made another profound difference in my health. I learned PGSG and Angel-Geschichte's 8 Field Qigong practice, which inspired me to revisit yoga since some of the forms are like yoga poses. After enduring years and years of fairly extreme spinal pain in my life, and with the doctors never seeming to be able to help me, I didn't know if I'd ever know life without pain. But after learning certain Qigong practices at the retreat, the physical pain in my body started to lessen. My joints felt better, and my spinal pain was diminishing. Most of all, I began to feel some joy and peace. I realized I had created so many different versions of myself based on traumas and illness. It was time to love all of these versions, offer compassion, and become whole. I can't help others out of their own flaming pits if I am still burning in my own.

Making the whole experience even more special, Steve journeyed to Washington with me and was able to have his own quiet time at the forests and beaches in the area. He was also able to attend the last night's program gathering with the group. It was very special for us both.

The retreat program was also inspiring for me. For the first time in my life, I was surrounded by people who never once judged me, people I could feel comfortable in my own skin with, people I could safely share pieces of my story without shame. They were willing to help bring my darkness to light and guide me about what to do with it once it surfaced. The funny thing was, I felt like I already knew them and that I had been in that place sometime before—before we even met. Once again,

I was offered new hope and a deeper transformation into myself, a place I had avoided for many years.

But as great as the whole experience was in itself, what was even more important was the fact that I could take home with me powerful and practical tools for a healthier, happier, and more peaceful life. It was a true rebirth.

After the retreat, I became laser-focused on healing. What I didn't know was that life was about to get really messy as I opened up my personal Pandora's box and began to bring light to the deep darkness that was hidden in my soul. I had stored it all away for my whole life, refusing to deal with it. I learned that I was only just beginning to peel layers of years of traumas. I realized that I had invested a lot of energy and time into negative thoughts, negative emotions, negative patterns, and self-pity into my illness and my life journey—and it needed to stop!

In September 2019, Steve and I traveled to Asheville, North Carolina, to meet Master Ou, attend his weekend workshop, and receive healing energy. It was a beautiful weekend. Steve and I met the hosts of the event, Anisha and Paul Fraser, who are long-time students of Master Ou. Anisha and Master Ou had also created something called Pangu Yoga, a gentle style of yoga that combines the benefits of yoga and the energy cultivation aspects of Qigong. So, I started to consider doing yoga again. I purchased the online video of Pangu Yoga from Anisha and started to add it to my daily practices. It helped me feel so much better. My nervous system began to calm down more, and I felt a tremendous amount of love and peace.

Next step, I felt God's gentle nudge to inquire about what I would need to do to teach Pangu Yoga, but I was resistant and had a lot of questions. So, I went into prayer about yoga and becoming a yoga instructor. My mind went wild: My perception was that it was a bad thing, and it wasn't "Christ-centered,"—basically, a lot of chatter from other people's opinions about religion. But that didn't feel true, so I persisted and reached out to Anisha for guidance. I began researching places where I could learn to become a yoga instructor, but felt no connection to any place in my area. So, I started looking for an organization that provided online learning. The only one I could find at that time was something called YogaFaith. This teaching changed my perspective about yoga. YogaFaith is about becoming Oneness with Christ, about surrender and devotion to Jesus Christ, and about embodying the body of Christ to fulfill your mission in life.

As I dove back into doing yoga again, I was a little intimidated at first because it had been so long. I could barely sit cross-legged in seated prayer posture on my mat without experiencing excruciating spinal and hip pain. The negative self-talk, "I am not good enough" attempted to win again, but I shut that door really quickly. I would not hear of it. Period. I kept getting that I must completely surrender my walk to the Lord. My focus was on obedience. Finally, after a lot of prayer, God opened the door in October 2019 to begin classes for me to become a Registered YogaFaith Trainer (R-YFT 200). I finally completed my YogaFaith Miracle Immersion October 2020. I continue to learn and reach new levels with YogaFaith. I am right where I am supposed to be on this day.

Ever since I went to the women's retreat with Angel and Keith, my healing practices have grown and accelerated, and they are a big part of who I am now. I now practice Pangu Shengong two to three hours a day. I had learned the "Moving Form" of the practice, which helps cultivate life force in the body. I have since learned the "Nonmoving Form" and the "Advanced Condensed Form" of Pangu Shengong, too. That effort has allowed me to go out in public without needing to shut down from the overwhelming energy surge I get from others around me. I don't always feel great when I practice the forms because the energy gets moved into places in my body that the illness and the traumas have debilitated. In fact, I often have to be present to what emotions come up as they point me in the direction of where I need more healing. But the process quiets my mind, helps me operate from a place of love, and be a light to others. The work has changed my life drastically and has, incredibly, made me excited about life again. What a gift!

In July 2020, I completed my first Pangu Shengong Moving Form Marathon with Master Ou and others from around the U.S. and the world. It took seven hours, so I wasn't quite sure if I would be able to complete it, but it felt important to help support my healing to wholeness of mind, body, spirit, and soul. I also did a 24-hour bone broth fast at the same time. By the end of it, I was completely exhausted, cold to touch but sweating profusely; my body ached from head to toe, I had numbness in my hands, and more—but I loved it because I was moving and cultivating an amazing God-given life force in my body. I look forward to possibly becoming a Pangu Shengong and a Pangu Yoga instructor in the future!

But there are other things I do every day, too, to enrich my healing besides these practices. I wake up every morning with gratitude. I am grateful that I still have my husband and my beautiful children who love me unconditionally. I give thanks to God for allowing me to be alive on this beautiful day, being a light to others in darkness, and being able to look in the mirror and say I love you to the person looking back at me.

When my mind wanders, I remind myself that I need to bring it back to finding gratitude and love in each situation regardless of how messy the situation is at the moment.

It's not uncommon for me to begin my day with up to four hours of prayer time on my yoga mat with Jesus, worship music, reading scripture, a devotion or two, praying in color (color as you pray), filling up journal pages from the Holy Spirit, Pangu Shengong, and just simply being still. When I'm on the road, I might only have an hour, but I also literally talk to God all day, privately or out loud with overflowing love and gratitude.

Plus, I've changed my attitude. I started becoming more aware of my thoughts, changing the words that I speak, and changing my environment if I find it isn't healthy for me. I made the decision to stop the complaining and letting my illness control my life. I made a promise to myself and God that when I have a negative thought, I will find the positive in it—regardless of the negative thought I'm thinking, what the doctor says, or what the person I see in the mirror or the photographs looks like. Healthy boundaries are important in healing. Now, more than ever and more than anything, I want peace.

I'm glad to say, too, that, although my mom and I have had our differences, we have been able to discuss and work through many of our issues throughout the years.

I've also incorporated several healing tools into my life to help me detox, balance, and strengthen my body. Once a week, when I'm not traveling, I use an Ionic Foot Detox, which helps to draw toxins from the body out through the feet. I use a far-infrared sauna, which uses light to create heat so you sweat out toxins. I started out doing it only once or twice a week; I had to start slowly and build myself up to be able to tolerate it.

The AmpCoil System caught my attention because the founders, Aaron Bigelow and his wife, are extremely passionate about helping those with health issues especially Lyme disease. It combines biofeedback and an electromagnetic coil to convey sound frequencies that harmonize, balance, and support wellness. It's one of my favorite tools over the years.

I also started using the ZAAZ Whole Body Vibration machine after leaving Mexico to help build my muscles and keep my lymphatics moving. It uses motion therapy to stimulate joints and muscles and reduce symptoms of circulatory problems and chronic pain. Since my chronic pain and the side effects of Lyme treatments had made it difficult for me to exercise, I started to lose a lot of muscle mass. I wanted to reverse that.

I was in search of a modality that I could use as a Traditional Naturopath, and I found XTRACT, which affects the lymphatic system primarily. But what really caught my attention about it was how it helps with emotional release, and I started to think it could be a way that I can help a lot of other people, too. I got very excited about it, so I jumped on a plane to California to work with the founder, Nina Venturella—and lo and behold, I had another spiritual experience. The minute Nina started working on my left side, I began sobbing and shaking uncontrollably. Then I heard, "The Holy Spirit is all over her. Give her time and space." The rest of that day was a blur.

Always researching for new ways to help myself, in 2018, I was scrolling in a Lyme Facebook community, and I came across a post that recommended a company called NES Health and had good things to say about their infoceutical products—solutions that are encoded with information that helps the body heal. I was especially interested because it said the products dealt with the body's energy fields. I knew that my body responds really well to energy healing and homeopathy, so I contacted them, got a scan, and was amazed at how accurate it was. I was so impressed with my results that I signed up to attend a training in Tampa, Florida, to become an NES practitioner. It was there that I met my now spiritual momma/mentor, Pamela, who has a very special place in my heart.

On top of all that, I started another program with Keith and Angel called Cultivate Life Force Health System, because I had accepted a field clerk position to work alongside my husband, and I wasn't sure how the stress of it would affect me. Sure enough, it has provided me with an extra boost of energy and healing.

So, in addition to the two to three hours of all forms of Pangu Shengong I do every day, my regimen includes YogaFaith practice, Pangu Yoga, my prayer/meditations, Cultivate Life Force Health System, Anisha's yoga classes, and NES Infoceuticals and Bach® Flower Remedies to help with emotions.

Of course, as much as has been healed in me, life is by no means perfect. I still struggle with spinal and back pain, especially when my Lyme flares up or if I am dealing with unresolved emotions. The yoga and stretching help tremendously. And, yes, I still struggle with symptoms from Lyme, but I remind myself that it's what I decide to do with them and how I choose to react to them that matters. Most of all, fear is not an option.

I've also tried a lot of special diets and eating regimens, but they were often confusing since there are so many opinions out there about anything you put in your mouth. I've found out there isn't a one-size-fits-all answer for everybody. I ate only plant-based foods for years—no sugar, no dairy, no processed foods, no sodas, lots of distilled water, lots of organic homemade bone broths, soups. I've tried it all. It's been a trial and error process to find out what my body can absorb and what it responds to best. It hasn't been easy. Now I do some intermittent fasting, and I occasionally fast up to 21 days for spiritual purposes, too. They seem to work best for me at this time.

Then—insult added to injury—I recently discovered a tick on my side and had to go to the ER to get it removed. Because of my history with Lyme, I wanted to make sure it was done right. But when I got to the ER, the nurse just about laughed in my face and told me I shouldn't be there; I didn't need to be there. She said it wasn't the kind of tick that carries Lyme, and that I could take care of it myself.

Her words were hurtful and truly traumatizing to me, so I started to walk out. She called me back in, asking what was wrong.

I turned to answer her. "Do you really want to know?" I asked her. "You don't know me, nor do I care if you do. I have lived through hell with Lyme and coinfections, I've been on my death bed many times, and I've been judged by people like you," I said, sobbing.

She softened and said, "Let me see it." She looked at it and pulled the dang tick out right there. "I just didn't want you to pay for an ER visit," she said.

"I understand," I told her, "and I'm grateful, but your behavior and attitude were hurtful and lacked compassion. I hope you or someone you love never has to go through this!"

When we got back to our hotel, Steve looked up the tick and found that it was known for carrying tick-related illnesses, Rocky Mountain Spotted Fever and Tularemia. I was proud that I took care of myself properly and didn't take people's judgments as I had done so much in the past. Now all I can do is make sure I stay on top of immune support, increase my Pangu Shengong practice, and pray that I have no serious repercussions from that day.

I know I have more work to do, and I will for the rest of my life, but it is worth it. I've made some pretty bad choices and decisions—many I am not so proud of. I have wallowed in a lot of shame and guilt over those years and suffered from it. But I am learning. In order to continue this path, I have to continue to eliminate the negative emotions and master my mindset. I have an open heart, and I choose to work through the triggers as they arise. I think the hardest battle is facing ourselves. It takes a warrior mindset to battle the lowest of the lowest thoughts. In our darkest moments, we find out what we are made of. I am learning to truly surrender, be obedient, and keep the faith—which carries me through. I am determined to live a life free of illness, and I will do the necessary work to get there. It's not an option. Life is precious!

My journey has birthed a new me. My life has changed, and I can't stop it—in a good way! My heart and my soul are opening, and I accept the truth that there is greatness in me, and I can use it to help others. The person I was no longer exists, and I'm much happier being the person I am becoming.

This new me owns her life and the struggles that went along with it. I do not let fear, worry, and doubt control me. I am beautiful, loved, and so much more. I used to hate me. I hated the way I looked and felt; I was just plain disgusted. I allowed people to run over me and accepted that I deserved it. I trusted people who were nothing but wolves in sheep's clothing. I've learned that if you rely on love from others, you will be disappointed every time. You cannot love or receive love if you don't start by loving yourself. And that allows you to receive the love that comes from the Father above.

I've learned to stop playing the victim/bully mentality over and over. I've realized I want to be a person who lives life to the fullest, who make choices that reflect what I want in life—not settle for the deck of cards I was dealt. I choose not to settle for anything less than I deserve in life anymore.

At some point in my childhood, my ability to express myself was shut down, and it stayed that way throughout most of my adult life. I was tainted by an extreme heaviness around having to live up to people's judgments and what they thought of me. Until now. Now, for the first time, I express myself. I am able to speak my truth in different ways that are unique to me. I express myself through writing, art, and my online boutique, mi-Chalet boutique. I am finding passions that stir my soul. I will never let anyone make me feel disempowered due to fear of confrontation and lack of confidence in myself. It's a very freeing experience.

I have learned on a deep level that love is the key. I often remind myself of Master Ou's words: "The more noble you love; the greater the healing." The more I heal my heart from all the pain, self-sabotage, abuse, and all of the garbage life has thrown at me, the happier I become, regardless of my circumstances. It is so easy to let life get in the way of your true self. But viewing everything with love allows me to see and listen differently—from the heart. It allows me to take in the energy to create, activate, and guide me into a more productive and powerful outcome. With love, I can heal the past, present, and future through this process, and I have learned that I can now also help others through their own healing process. The Lord has blessed me with some pretty amazing gifts; there's no need to fear them anymore.

As I've done my work, my relationship with God has become unbreakable. Prayer provided me comfort in my life for many years, but for much of that time, I'd get frustrated with God because nothing seemed to be happening as a result. My challenges and pain caused me to question my heart and my faith; for a long time, even my hope was destroyed. I just about gave up at one point, but God continued to open and close doors for me because He knows what is best. I finally recognized that I have to trust and stay rooted in His word. I had to come empty. No more old beliefs, mindsets, patterns, perceptions, doubts, and fears. I had a choice—either to let this dis-ease kill me or to take control and take my life back. Find a way. I started to understand that He has me in the palm of His hand. That there is nothing to fear. I am still here because of a greater purpose in life. I finally began to realize that God uses the broken; I have been called to live with intention, to be a beacon of light in the darkness, and to help those who have lost all hope.

The journey has circled me back to my true identity in Christ—that I am the daughter of the Most High. He is my Father and loves me unconditionally and provides me mercy and grace and the gift that my sins have all been forgiven. I now live my life to please Him, not people. At the end of the day, He passes judgment, not the human flesh. My strength comes from Him. He knows my heart and that is *all* that matters!

The Holy Spirit speaks to me, each day, in a very gentle reveal of the next layer to be released or more work to be done on a previous layer. I am here today because I have been given a second chance at life. I want to live out the rest of my days doing His will and what He has called me to do. I have been searching for a purpose for a long time. My soul has been restored.

I also seem to have a very close connection to the angelic realms, and, over the years, I often have dreams where they speak to me and give me messages. It's even become somewhat common for me to leave my body and find myself in dreams with Archangel Michael. I'm usually dressed in dull and dingy full-metal armor, often in a battle fighting evil and saving souls. Then, I'd often be told, "You have much training to do, my child." I would wake up the next morning feeling as if I hadn't slept at all. I was beginning to get a sense that I was put on this earth to help in some way beyond what I fully understood.

In one dream, I was riding in the back of a beat-up pickup truck in the middle of the desert with Archangel Michael. He turned to me and said, "I have to show you something," and a multitude of dreamy scenes flicked quickly past us. I kept saying, "Can we slow down? I can't keep up." Then there was silence and just a smile from Michael. I continued to ask: "What is this? Who is this? We are going too fast; I can't see." Michael said, "Patience, my child. You will see soon enough."

Finally, I saw in front of us a naked woman lying in "child's pose," in complete surrender, with the most beautiful, intricate, detailed white wings. She was so mesmerizing, beautiful, and delicate, yet strong. I felt so drawn to touch her. I got out of the truck and slowly walking to her, almost in a trance. I kneeled down beside her and asked, "Is she real? Who is she?" Michael said, "That is you, my child! This is your Awakening: Truth Be Told. Darkness no longer resides. Only light and love."

And, as I am guided, *"Awakening: Truth Be Told"* will be the name of my next book!

In another dream I had in 2019, Jesus carried me to the beach and laid my body in the water while waves were crashing over me. I was rebaptized and given strict instructions of ministry, where I was to help and guide others to wholeness, share hope, and let others know that "broken" can still be beautiful. I was told that I would be sharing my story, as painful as it is, to help others fight for the light within themselves.

I walk in obedience and follow the path that has been set forth; I will never feel I am walking it alone.

We live in a very negative world consumed by darkness. I have seen that we have become so consumed by our hurts and other people's opinions, but we already have it inside of us to hear our own voices and be liberated. We are being held captive by our own belief systems and playing the blame game, but no one—and I mean no one—is responsible for our peace and happiness. We have to ask ourselves, where am I placing my energy? What is of highest priority? Freedom is a choice. Every single moment of the day can be a new beginning. Take things as they come and truly deal with them and let them go—don't sweep them under the rug and let the misery build up. Let your true self rise out of the flames. We have it in our very souls to do so.

I want to say a few words to you, my reader, to pass my torch of healing to you because you are worth it. It is important to remember that you are beautiful. You are healed. You are intelligent. You are loved. You are free. You are deserving. You are the child of the Most High. And simply, you are who God called you to be. Don't resist; embrace. The purpose of this life is to love yourself, know yourself, and trust yourself. It is to set your soul free and see others in a higher light.

I never settle on trying to heal. Giving up is not an option now in my life. There's a will; there's a way. Many of us don't take time to recognize just how much life is a precious gift. Each moment presents an opportunity, and it is up to us with what we do and think about it. Positive and negative emotions will show themselves; be mindful in the present moment on how you respond to them. Be willing to receive the blessings from above.

I wrote this poem as I sat on my yoga mat after studying YogaFaith Trauma-Sensitive material in one of my own "Be Still and Listen" prayer sessions. I asked, *"What is it that you are speaking to my heart, Lord?"* And this is what I wrote:

The Seas

Complete darkness rages around
Feeling like I am bound
Evil lurks in the storm
This cannot be the norm.

Where am I
Who am I
Can this be
I see Jesus now looking at me.

A faint whisper I hear
You must know I am always near
See the light in the distance
It's called hope and met with persistence

One step my precious child
There is no love like mine
I will carry you through
Until you are completely healed and made anew.

Michelle L. Potter
April 23, 2020

Printed in the United States
by Baker & Taylor Publisher Services